# The Public Prayer Station

*Taking Healing Prayer to the Streets and Evangelizing the Nones*

The Rev. William L. De Arteaga

Emeth Press
www.emethpress.com

*The Public Prayer Station: Taking Healing Prayer to the Streets and Evangelizing the Nones*

Copyright © 2018 William L. De Arteaga

Printed in the United States of America on acid-free paper. All rights reserved. No part of this book may be reproduced, or stored in a retrieval system or transmitted in any form or by any means, electronic, mechanical, photocopying, recording, scanning or otherwise, except as permitted by the 1976 United States Copyright Act, or with the prior written permission of Emeth Press. Requests for permission should be addressed to: Emeth Press, P. O. Box 23961, Lexington, KY 40523-3961. http://www.emethpress.com.

ISBN 978-1-60947-141-5
Library of Congress Control Number: 2018959999

For my wife Carolyn, who supported my research and writing since we were first married over four decades ago. She never said "Why don't you get a REAL job and make good money?" And for the many Facebook friends who prayed for the success of this work.

# Table of Contents

**Introduction / ix**

**Part I: Pioneering the Public Prayer Station / 1**

    1. How the Holy Spirit inspired the first Public Prayer Station / 3

    2. Discovering the Hunter's innovations in healing prayer / 13

    3. At Little Five Points / 23

    4. Public Prayer Stations on the run / 31

    5. Deliverance in the park / 41

**Part II: Taking the Public Prayer Stations to the World / 49**

    6. YWAM and spread the ministry / 51

    7. Chairs as the public prayer station / 57

**Part III: Starting a public prayer station / 65**

    8. Ready, shoot, aim! / 67

**Resources / 71**

**Appendix / 75**

# Introduction

> "When you enter a town and are welcomed, eat what is offered to you. Heal the sick who are there and tell them, 'The kingdom of God has come near to you.'
> – Luke 10:8-9

On a warm and sunny Saturday afternoon, back in 1987, the first recorded public prayer station began at a pedestrian walkway and mini-park at "Little Five Points" in Atlanta, Georgia. Four prayer intercessors volunteered to go and do that experimental ministry. The place chosen had shade trees and a park bench, and was adjacent to a pizza shop. We intercessors brought along a repainted real estate sign on a wooden base, with the words "Prayer Station" in large red letters (picture, p. 38). Carolyn, my wife, and I stood next to the sign and began greeting the passers-by, "Hi, would you like prayer today for any intention or healing?" The other two intercessors sat down at the bench a few yards from the sign, ready to come up and join in as needed.

That afternoon we prayed for over a dozen persons, with varied intentions such as new job opportunities, to healing from major diseases. An especially memorable prayer event happened as a group of four young women passed through. One was on crutches with her left leg in a cast from her toe to just below the knee, and I asked her what was the issue with her leg. "I broke my ankle playing tennis." Her tone and expression showed disdain. I asked, "Does it hurt still?" "Some," she answered. "How about some healing prayer on that leg?" I asked. "Sure, give it your best shot, preacher." Again, in a sour and dismissive tone.

"OK, fine," I said. Two intercessors from the bench joined us. I bent over and touched the cast at the ankle area, and the other two intercessors began praying also. I prayed using the command mode that is normative to the New Testament, but was uncommon and controversial at that time (discussed in detail in chapter 2). "In Jesus' name, I speak to the ankle area. I command every fractured bone to re-knit and be healed. I command all swelling to subside, and every muscle, tendon and the entire area to return to health and normality. I speak to the pain and command it to leave now – in Jesus' name."

The girl had a puzzled look. I asked, "Less pain?" She delayed and said, "No pain." I suggested, "Why don't you try gently touching it to the ground." She did so and her look changed to astonishment. Without prompting she stepped harder, and then stomped on the ground.

"Wow! You guys are for real. It's OK... no pain, nothing. This is real!' The other three girls looked on in amazement, and began smiling. The girl with the healed ankle repeated, "You guys are for real. Thank you, thank you! Oh thank you very much."

They moved on, and about thirty minutes later came back, with some shopping bags full of stuff. I was praying with another person with a back problem and doing a leg extension (see chapter 2) and did not speak to them again, but they had a conversation with one of the other intercessors. It turns out that the girl in the cast was a "preacher's kid" from a denomination that did not believe in healing. She often ridiculed the TV healing evangelists as phonies and charlatans. Sadly, she had not been in any church for several years. So the Lord had just given her a lesson in the reality of healing prayer – and the Gospels.

On that first outing three persons were led to the Lord by our intercessor team. I personally led one. A young man came for prayer for a "broken heart." He had just broken up with his girl-friend. Carolyn, who is a licensed counselor and especially good at inner healing prayer, prayed that the Lord would heal his emotions, and bring to him the person just right for him. I asked if he had accepted Jesus as Lord. The young man said, "No," and further, "Yes," he would like to receive Jesus as Lord and savior. I led him through the sinner's prayer. His demeanor turned to joy. I reminded him to follow up and go back to his home church and read the Bible daily. He had not been in there for years, but promised he would.

These two cases that summer day show the promise and worth of the public prayer station ministry. It demonstrates the Gospel and brings the Kingdom of God via healing and prayer to persons who may not normally go to church. Of course persons who are church goers are also ministered to, but the salient issue here is that "Nones" (non-affiliated and non-church goers) can be effectively reached and touched by this ministry.

A note about the term "public prayer station:"

For this book I have coined the term "public prayer station" and its acronym (PPS). This is to avoid confusion with the other uses of the term "prayer station" as a place *within* a church or church grounds where Christians come to pray. For example, some churches place pictures of police and firemen, schools, the White House, etc., along a wall in their church where church members can come and intercede in prayer for the things pictured, as in, for instance, the safety of their police and firemen, or for wisdom for government officials. These are also called "prayer stations."

This is a recent innovation of the last decades and a splendid encouragement to the Christians' duty to intercessory prayer (1 Tim 2:2). It may be considered a variation of the traditional "stations of the cross" found in Roman Catholic and other liturgical churches which picture Jesus´ suffering and crucifixion on Good Friday. These all have in common the fact that they are in a church or designated church space where Christians come to pray.[1] These church prayer stations are not fundamentally evangelistic in intent.

The public prayer station (PPS), on the other hand, is situated in a public, non-church place, where both Christians and non-Christians pass by. The PPS is intrinsically more evangelical. That is, it presents the prayer power of the Kingdom of God to many who are not Christian or have had little experience with effective healing and intercessory prayer. As cited in the young man with the "broken heart," the PPS is often the setting for an invitation to receive Christ for a person who has just received effective healing prayer.

---

[1] Just one example of the many in-church prayer stations that can be found on the web is this one encouraging the virtue of courage, which is used in youth camps: Sara Hargreaves, "Courage Prayer Stations," *Engage Worship*, Posted June 15, 2016. https://engageworship.org/ideas/courage-prayer-stations

# Part I

# Pioneering the Public Prayer Station

# 1

# How the Holy Spirit inspired the first Public Prayer Station

The ministry of the public prayer station (PPS) has now reached many countries, from North and Latin America, and even "Down Under" in Australia and New Zealand. But launching the first PPS was not the result of long planning and high expectation. Rather this ministry came about almost accidentally (but really *providentially*). The Holy Spirit prepared a group of us to begin this innovative and new ministry without our considering it as of great significance or impact.

Back in 1985, I was placed in leadership of a group of prayer intercessors at an Episcopal church, St. Patrick's of Dunwoody (North Atlanta). They were really wonderful intercessors and "prayer warriors." Their principal duty was to serve as prayer intercessors for healing and other needs as the Sunday service ended. I wanted to do something more with them than pray at church on Sundays. At the time I was a layperson and relatively new to both the Episcopal Church and to the gifts of the Holy Spirit.

In fact, just six years earlier I was an atheist, trying to live a "swinging singles" life – very far from the Lord indeed. Ironically, I had grown up a devote Catholic, in the traditional Catholicism of the 1950's. But like all my Catholic friends, I never saw a miracle of healing or any other kind, although the nuns and brothers at parochial school told us many stories of saints' miracles in the past. I believed the stories, and as a boy I took the Catholic faith extremely seriously. I recall being upset that my Dad watched and enjoyed a Billy Graham sermon on TV. After all, that man was a *heretic*!

When family members or friends were sick we went to church for prayer and lit a candle for their healing. I don't recall ever having that type of prayer answered unambiguously, as in a healing that was medically impossible or unexpected. The laying on of hands on the sick in faith was beyond our imagination. In 1957, when I was in the seventh grade, my older brother had a sports accident which left him with a blood clot in the leg. It broke out and killed him. In his last hours, as his heart was closing down, a priest came to his bedside and administered the sacrament of "extreme unction." Catholics believed that from this sacrament he would avoid the pains of Purgatory and go immediately to heaven. Not a word was said during the rite for his physical healing, nor had any words or the laying on of hands been done on him in his month at the hospital.[1]

Like almost all Christians in the 1950s, Catholics were operating in a huge biblical and ministry gap, but totally unaware of these lacks. The Christian faith, as defined biblically, not only pertains to doctrines, personal prayers and participation in church worship, but should manifest "signs and wonders," including miraculous healings, in a continuous loop of faith verification and spiritual practice.

> This salvation, which was first announced by the Lord, was confirmed to us by those who heard him. God also testified to it by *signs, wonders and various miracles, and by gifts of the Holy Spirit* distributed according to his will. (Heb 2:2-4)

Further, these supernatural events should be ministered in the local church thru *all* its members (1 Cor 12-14). Anything short of that may be "normal," but it is *sub-biblical*.[2]

This ministry and knowledge gap was also present in the Protestant churches, perhaps even more so. Protestants did not generally believe or

---

[1] In my earlier book, *Quenching the Spirit* (Lake Mary: Creation House, 1996) I described how the sacrament of anointing with oil for healing (James 5) had been debased in the Middle Ages to become a "skip Purgatory" ritual – a very great loss. The priest who ministered extreme unction on my brother was a family friend and a wonderful priest, Fr. Ivan Illich. He later achieved fame as a revolutionary of educational theory with his book, *Deschooling Society* (New York: Harper& Row, 1972). But neither he nor the other Catholic priests of the era understood or practiced effective, biblically modeled healing prayer.

[2] In my work, *Agnes Sanford and Her Companions: The Assault on Cessationism and the Coming of the Charismatic Renewal* (Eugene: Wipf & Stock, 2015) I call this sub-biblical mode of Christianity the "Augustinian consensus" to indicate that since the Fourth Century the Church became accustomed to functioning without the gifts of the Spirit and has believed that to be normal.

celebrate the miracles of their own saints and heroes of faith, such as Pastor Johann Blumhardt (1805-1880) of Germany. That pastor preformed many exorcisms and healing miracles at both his parish church and at a healing spa he established, but his work was marginalized and ignored.[3] Effective healing prayer, and the miraculous and the gifts of the Spirit, were all quenched by the awful Protestant doctrine of "cessationism" which claimed that those gifts and supernatural events ceased with the death of the Apostles.[4]

Practically the only Christians doing effective healing in the 1950s were the "crazy" Pentecostals. We Catholics and Protestants did not agree on many things, but one thing we were sure of was that the Pentecostals were cultic, hyper-emotional and their healing claims bogus and not worth considering—for sure.

My personal descent into atheism happened three years after graduating from Fordham University in 1966. There I learned a lot of Catholic theology and philosophy, but much of it was infused with trendy Protestant liberal theology (cessationist) which discounted the miraculous, including the biblical miracles. With me, as with many others, this sapped the belief in the Bible as the Word of God, and atheism or agnosticism replaced my youthful faith. I spent five years as an atheist "ex-Catholic" before I returned to belief in God through a series of dreams (1974).[5]

After several weeks as a "re-born" Believer, I had a strange and wonderful experience as I lay in bed praying. I felt waves of energy coming into my body through my hands, and I knew it was God's doing. Like Peter before Jesus after the miracle of the net full of fishes (Lk 5:6-8) the first thing I mumbled was, "Depart from me for I am a sinful man." But the Lord did not, and I discovered I had a gift of healing via the lying on of hands. I made contact with a Catholic charismatic group and there further experienced "signs and wonders" that activated the loop of faith and experiences every Christian should know.

The leader of the Catholic charismatic group suggested we go to a Full Gospel Businessmen's Fellowship International (FGBMFI) breakfast at a local hotel. We went and I was astounded by several things. First, the

---

[3]Friedrich Zundel, *The Awakening: One Man's Battle With Darkness* (Walden: Plough, 2000).

[4]A very detailed critique of cessationsim is Jon Ruthven's *On the Cessation of the Charismata: The Protestant Polemic on Post-Biblical Miracles* (Tulsa: Word & Spirit, 1993) I discuss the tragic rise of cessationism and its central role in Protestant Christianity in both *Quenching the Spirit* and *Agnes Sandford and Her Companions*

[5]I tell this story in more detail in my work, *Forgotten Power: The Significance of the Lord's Supper in Revivals* (Grand Rapids: Zondervan, 2003) Chapter 2.

intense level of verifiable spiritual activity as the guest evangelist prayed for healing needs of those attending. Most had instant healings, including myself from arthritis in the neck that had not dispersed even after several prayer attempts.

The second impressive fact was the love and ecumenical unity in the group. These were dedicated denominational folks, Catholics, Presbyterians, Methodists, Baptists, etc., but it made no difference as they fellowshipped and prayed with and for each other. I thought to myself, "Four hundred years ago they would have tried to kill each other." In terms of classical theology, they were heretical to each other, especially along the Roman Catholic and Baptist divide.[6] But God did not seem to mind, and we were all being blessed and healed, and enjoying each other's fellowship as we witnessed about healing and miracles that had occurred recently.[7]

I determined that although I would remain a Catholic, I would investigate how these other denominations, and especially how the "crazy" Pentecostals had come to the knowledge of effective healing and the gifts of the Sprit way before we Catholics or the mainline Protestants. A local Pentecostal church, Mt. Paran Church of God, had a reputation for both being very charismatic and having great preaching. I began going to that church's Sunday evening services, while still going to Catholic mass in the morning.

Quickly, I became a "charismaniac," and began devouring the new charismatic literature that was pouring out then. I read the Catholic authors such as Fr. Frances MacNutt and Fr. Michael Scanlon, but also Pentecostal authors such as Derek Prince, Kenneth Hagin, and charismatic Episcopalians such as Dennis Bennett. Cassette ministries were popular in the 1970s, and I listened to one tape after another from such charismatic leaders as Agnes Sanford, Glenn Clark and Tommy Tyson. I wanted to learn everything I could about the healing ministry and the Spirit-filled life.

One healing conference I attended was sponsored by the Order of St. Luke (OSL). This was founded in the 1930's by Episcopalians, but even

---

[6] My wife had learned in Sunday Bible school that those who were not Baptists went to hell, and I learned just the opposite in Catholic School.

[7] I have suggested that the founding of the FGBMFI in the 1950s is really the beginning of the Charismatic Renewal, rather than the dramatic incident at St. Paul' in California in 1960 when the Episcopal rector, Denis Bennett, announced he spoke in tongues. See my article, "Demos Shakarian and his Ecumenical Businessmen," *Pneuma Review.* Posted August 4, 2014. http://pneumareview.com/demos-sakarian-and-the-his-ecumenical-businessmen/

from its founding, totally ecumenical.[8] It stressed the healing ministry of the church through the sacraments, but also through lay persons in the laying on of hands. This was revolutionary in the 1930s in the mainline churches, and too close to Pentecostalism for most traditional Christians. But the OSL gained a few footholds among Episcopal and other mainline churches.[9]

From the start of my entry into charismatic Christianity I was not shy about offering prayers in public or at my work place to any who needed it. I gained the reputation of being a "fanatic" at my workplace, but when anyone needed prayer they came to me – strangely enough.

At Mt. Paran Church of God I met a lovely lady, Carolyn Koontz, and we began dating. Our first meeting was at a restaurant with some singles from an evening Bible study. As I walked her to her car she complained that she had a migraine headache. I laid hands on her head and prayed, and it went away. She told me later that she was in dread of any of her friends seeing such "weird" behavior. During our first date a waitress spilled hot coffee on her hand. I prayed right then and there for her healing by laying my hands over the scorched and reddened area, and her hand was immediately healed.

Carolyn was initially embarrassed at these public displays of prayer, but astounded and delighted by the immediate healing result. She had been raised as a devout Baptist (and cessationist) and like myself never saw a healing miracle. Several weeks later something similar happened at a horse show where I prayed for a young girl who had fallen off her horse and badly sprained her arm.[10] The week after that I invited Carolyn to come with me to a deliverance session I was scheduled to do, and there she awoke to the fact that she had the gift of discernment of spirits as she called out the names of the spirits afflicting the person. (Singles, are you attentive? A "dinner and an exorcism" date is a great way to woo someone you are interested in.) Carolyn and I married in January of 1979.

---

[8] On the history and development of the OSL see my blog posting: "The Anglican Tradition of Healing: Part II, the OSL," *Anglican Pentecostal.* Posted, Sept. 9, 2013. http://anglicalpentecostal.blogspot.com/2013/09/the-anglican-tradition-in-healing-part.html

[9] It should be noted that another para-Church group, the Camps Furthest Out, (CFO) was even more important in spreading healing, inner healing and the new Pentecostalism among the mainline churches. I discuss the importance of both groups in *Agnes Sanford and Her Companions.*

[10] The incident is described in Carolyn's book, *Watching God Work: The Stuff of Miracles* (Painesville: Bridge-Logos, 2014).

Carolyn had been abandoned by her husband for another woman and was now divorced. Because the Catholic Church would not recognize any valid reason for divorce, I could not receive communion at my Catholic Church. We moved to the Episcopal Church, and landed at St. Patrick's as our parish church. That church was for decades a dynamite charismatic congregation – something like Mt. Paran. Its rector, the Rev. Gray Temple, was educated in the liberal theological tradition, but he had a dramatic encounter with the demonic which informed him that much of his liberal theology was wrong about this issue.[11] Like me, he quickly read up on the current charismatic literature on healing and the demonic – the very things that seminary had ignored.[12]

Carolyn and I joined the OSL chapter at St. Patrick's. Like other OSL groups, we met twice a month after Sunday services, shared a pot-luck meal and discussed new books or topics on healing and deliverance issues. At St. Patrick's the OSL was also responsible to train and schedule the church prayer intercessors for healing and other intentions. At the Sunday services, two OSL teams were posted at the side of the sanctuary. After people received communion they had the option of going to one of the intercession stations for prayer. Many churches now do that, but at the time, St. Patrick's was one of the leaders of this. It was a very effective ministry, and some persons from other churches came to St. Patrick's just for this healing touch.

A year after we came to St. Patrick's the OSL convener (chairperson) moved out of state and I was elected to take her place. I continued the pattern of twice monthly meetings, and did my best to bring in speakers of interest. Inner healing was gaining great attention with the best-selling books by Ruth Carter Stapleton, the sister of President Carter, and we had several speakers on that ministry.[13] Among the speakers there was one who was using inner healing to minister to persons with homosexual attractions. The classic book on this specialized ministry, *The Broken Image* had just come out.[14] That ministry was and continues to be especially controversial, and ultimately led to my separation from St. Patrick's (see

---

[11] A taped interview of Fr. Gray, describing his hair-raising encounter with the demonic realm is in the author's possession.

[12] I wrote about how thoroughly and tragically most seminaries avoid and obstruct the knowledge of the ministry of healing and deliverance in, *Agnes Sanford and Her Companions*, chapter 23.

[13] Ruth Carter Stapleton, *The Gift of Inner Healing* (Waco: Word Books, 1976). Her books are OK on inner healing case studies, but weak on theology. For a balanced presentation of inner healing it is best to consult, John Sandford, and Paula Sandford, *The Transformation of the Inner Man* (South Plainfield, Bridge, 1982).

[14] Leanne Payne, *The Broken Image* (Grand Rapids: Cornerstone Books, 1981).

next chapter). But aside from this innovation, and the Hunter's discoveries, which can be taught quickly (discussed below) healing and deliverance ministry are plainly described in the New Testament. Education in the healing and deliverance ministries mainly means re-educating a person from the terrible theology of cessationism, or the Roman Catholic variety, that only the saints and very holy persons can minister healing prayer. I call this latter error the "Galatian bewitchment," from Gal 3:1-6.[15]

The truth is that new information on healing is hard to come by. At the time I was doing research on the renewed Christian healing movement of the early Twentieth Century and I was struck by the fact that the pioneer books on Christian healing such as Pearcy Dearmer's *Body and Soul*, or F. Bosworth's *Christ the Healer*, were little different in content or insights from the books coming out in the Charismatic Renewal.[16] What to teach and do with this fine OSL group? Teaching about confidentiality in the healing ministry for the third time gets boring.

The answer came into focus in 1986 when I stumbled on the new book by John Wimber (1934- 1997) founder of the Vineyard Fellowship, called *Power Evangelism*.[17] Wimber was raised in an atheistic family that for three generations had never been to church, – a "none" in current terminology. He investigated a local Quaker home Bible study because he was having marital trouble and thought they might help. He quickly accepted Christ there and became enthusiastically evangelical – his marriage was also healed in that Bible study. In the process he read and re-read the Bible and discovered he had a gift for personal evangelization.

After a year, he decided he would investigate what "church going" was all about. He went to a nearby Baptist Church and was very disappointed. The music was awful (he was a professional musician) and the sermon boring. After the service, he went to the pastor and asked, "When do you do the stuff?"

The pastor replied, "What stuff?" Wimber, "You know, the stuff in the Bible, like healing the sick and casting out demons." "Oh," he replied, "We don't do that anymore, although sometimes we sing about it."[18] Wim-

---

[15]*Agnes Sanford and Her Companions*, chapter 1, "The Early Church."

[16]Pearcy Dearmer's, *Body and Soul* (New York; E.P. Dutton & Co., 1909). F.F. Bosworth, *Christ the Healer* (Chosen, 2009), first edition, 1920.

[17]John Wimber, and Kevin Springer, *Power Evangelism* (San Francisco: Harper Collins, 1986)

[18]There are variations in the exact wording and sequence of this famous encounter, See the discussion of this incident done in mock "higher criticism" mode of biblical scholars trying to source one of Jesus' saying, in Peter Hocken, *Azusa Rome and Zion* (Pickwick: 2016) chapter 2.

ber accepted this cessationist explanation and became a dedicated Baptist pastor, but he was restless about the disconnect between the Biblical narrative and present zero miraculous practice. In a story we have not the space to relate, he came to understand that cessationism was wrong, and the gifts of the Sprit are active today for those who have the faith to receive them. The denomination he founded, the Vineyard Fellowship, was and continues to be fully charismatic and famous for "doing the stuff" of the Bible.[19]

Wimber stressed bold evangelism, as in praying for people where you encountered their need or hurt. He believed this should be done even in the marketplace or office, just as in the Book of Acts. I was already doing that, but his *Power Evangelism* prodded me into thinking about how to do "the stuff" more *systematically* with the OSL group. I prayed about it and the Lord gave me the phrase, "prayer station."

I knew of "Stations of Cross" as a Catholic, but these were in church, focused on Jesus' crucifixion, and had nothing to do with healing prayer or evangelism. So I knew the Lord meant something else. Our OSL chapter had less than $80 in its treasury, so we could not buy a vacated gas station a few blocks from the church. So, "What else, Lord?" As I walked my dog I noticed a real estate sign planted on a home's front lawn, and it reminded me of a traditional station of the cross, but it was in public, and at the edge of a busy sidewalk. Hey, so maybe...?

I discussed this idea with the OSL group at St. Patrick's and they were all for trying it.[20] But where? America was no longer a pedestrian country. And Atlanta in particular is a "drive to" city. If we sat up the prayer station sign in front of our church the people would just wiz by. Someone suggested the Bohemian and hippy section in downtown Atlanta called "Little Five Points." It had many tourist boutiques and a lot of pedestrian traffic. That sounded interesting and the next Saturday Carolyn and I went down to investigate.

---

[19]Ironically, Wimber wanted an easy-going form of Pentecostalism, with less emphasis on tongues and less outbursts of phenomenon such as slaying in the spirit. God's irony and humor were visited upon the Vineyard as its churches became centers of revival where much phenomena were in manifestation. In fact, The Toronto Airport Vineyard was the focus of a large and influential revival in the 1990s that had many controversial phenomena such as "animal sounds." This became a point of contention between Wimber and the Toronto Vineyard pastor, John Arnott. Arnott separated his congregation for the Vineyard fellowship ad continued his sometimes free-wheeling revival sessions.

[20]This was 30 years ago, and I don't remember the names of many of the members in that OSL group. But unforgettable was Miss Lynda Wynn, a petit and beautiful woman who had been at one time the fiancé of Senator Sam Nunn of Georgia. She has already gone to her eternal reward

It was ideal. There was a mini-park with several benches and shady trees just adjacent to a sidewalk. Besides a pizza place and café, there was an occult book store and a metaphysical supply store selling charms and crystals all within view of the park. I thought, "This place really needs ministry." As St. Paul wrote, "But where sin abounded, grace did much more abound." (Rm 5:20).

We met a policeman on the beat. I described the prayer station idea and he said there was no law against it as long as it did not obstruct normal traffic. Our prayer station sign would be small, so there was no problem. (Later, we wound up praying for his safety and intentions multiple times). I had a real estate sign from the sale of the house we bought that the agent never collected. I painted it over in a beige color. I also had a 2 by 4 section of lumber and formed an "H" base for the sign.[21] I then lettered the sign "Prayer Station" and painted a cross at the top. Given the neighborhood we were going to, I wanted to be clear that it was not a Buddhist, New Age or Hare Krishna prayer station. I also wrote in smaller letters, "Let us minister to you in prayer."

---

[21]Years later an engineer looked at it and complimented me on the economy, stability and soundness of the base design (the Holy Spirit designed it with the only material I had on hand.

*12    The Public Prayer Station*

Some of the OSL PPS volunteers from St. Patrick's.
Carolyn is in the center next to yours truly.
The ID badges we used is clearly seen on the woman on the left.
Picture in author's possession.

The rector of St. Patrick's, Fr. Gray, liked our idea. He asked only that the intercessors wear some sort of identification that they belonged to the OSL. Plastic ID badges from Office Depot solved that. We also agreed that the intercessor group would be specifically blessed and prayed over for this ministry the next Sunday. That was August 16th, 1987. We were blessed and anointed by Fr. Gray and his assistant priest as the whole congregation extended their hands in blessing and prayer.

We went to Little Five Points the next Saturday, August 22, packing a foam ice chest full of soft drinks. There were four of us. My wife and I and two other intercessors. We wanted to see if this would work.

We will get to a further description of the two marvelous and grace filled summers we held the PPS further on. But I want to describe one last, and important element that made our prayer station especially effective in ministering healing prayer. That is, the discoveries of the Pentecostal couple, Charles and Frances Hunter, and of how to pray more effectively and quickly for the sick.

# 2

# Discovering the Hunter's innovations in healing prayer

Early in 1986, about six months before going out on our first prayer station, Carolyn and I ran into persons who were praying for the sick in what seemed to be an unusual manner – by command. They would say things like, "In Jesus' name, I command the spirit of arthritis out, and normality to be restored to this knee," as they laid hands on the person.[1] This command mode is the normative New Testament way for healing prayer, but it had been long forgotten and explained away as irrelevant for the current age. It seemed to us as something only Jesus or an Apostle could do. This command mode is different from the petition mode which is normative to most contemporary Christians. For instance, "Father, in Jesus' name, heal this arthritic knee." Petition prayers for healing are found in the Psalms and other sections of the Old Testament, and are certainly valid and effective. But they are not found in the New Testament for any form of healing or deliverance situation.

We were introduced to the command form of prayer when we were invited to attend a healing course taught by a saintly elderly couple, Zeb and Maida Burnett (both have gone to be with the Lord). They taught from the materials developed by Charles and Frances Hunter, a Pentecostal couple who brought command healing to world-wide attention (more on them below). The Burnetts held their sessions at a non-denominational charismatic church, Christ Church, that was near our own church.

---

[1] This chapter is based on my earlier blog posting "The Hunter's Revolution in Healing Ministry," *The Anglican Pentecostal*. Posted May 8, 2013. http://anglicalpentecostal.blogspot.com/2013/05/the-hunters-revolution-in-healing.html

The Burnetts' eight-session course was a model of good teaching and organization. It included hand-outs, a binder, mandatory readings, and many practice prayer exercises. Before being given a certificate of completion we had to view fifteen hours of videos, read the two principal Hunter books on healing, *How to Heal the Sick*, and *Handbook of Healing*.[2] We were tested on all the materials.

When we came to the course, Carolyn and I had already learned much about healing prayer from classic Pentecostal and charismatic teachers, such as Derik Prince, Fr. Frances MacNutt, and others, both at their conferences, and through their books and tapes. We were grateful for all of these, but we became convinced the Hunter insights were both soundly biblical and often more effective than the traditional petition prayers that had been modeled for us.

Before going further, let me briefly cite the New Testament scriptures on this, because it is still unfamiliar to many Christians. Command healing was apparently done by the disciples from their first commissioning when Jesus sent them into the countryside of Judea: "The seventy-two returned with joy and said, "Lord, even the demons submit to us in your name." (Lk 10:17) Although we have no descriptions of exactly how the seventy-two ministered to the sick and demon possessed, it is significant that they were amazed by their *authority*. They said nothing about the elegance of their prayers, etc. So whatever they said to chase out the demons rested on their authority as disciples of Jesus and the use of his name.

From earliest times Christians have practiced the exorcism of evil spirits as a direct command to the malignant entity, but past Apostolic times commands for healing were not used regularly. This is particularly unfortunate because all the accounts of healings recorded in Acts were ministered through commands. For example, when Peters saw the lame beggar near the Temple:

> Then Peter said, "Silver or gold I do not have, but what I have I give you. In the name of Jesus Christ of Nazareth, walk." Taking him by the right hand, he helped him up, and instantly the man's feet and ankles became strong. (Acts 3: 6-7)

---

[2]Charles Hunter, and Frances Hunter, *How to Heal the Sick* (Kingwood: Hunter books, 1981), and, Charles Hunter, and Frances Hunter, *Handbook of Healing: Supplement to How to Heal the Sick* (Kingwood, TX: Hunter Books, 1987). I have modeled my own healing workshop on the Burnett's, although shortened to one day. See a description of this abbreviated workshop in, *The Anglican Pentecostal*, "Church of the Redeemer: Healing Workshop." Posted, October 27, 2017. https://www.blogger.com/blogger.g?blogID=4318439059531993933#editor/target=post;postID=6717115488962699944

Command healing in Jesus' name was not just a prerogative of the Apostles, as some commentators claim. We see the command healing mode described in Paul's retelling in Jerusalem of his healing from the blindness he suffered, when he first met the risen Lord on the road to Damascus.

> "A man named Ananias came to see me. He was a devout observer of the law and highly respected by all the Jews living there. He stood beside me and said, `Brother Saul, receive your sight!' And at that very moment I was able to see him." (Acts 22:12-13)

Note the command mode. How and why the post-Apostolic Christians drifted into healing via petition prayer has not been examined, but it certainly must be understood as part of the general decline of the healing ministry that took place from the Third Century on. Christians in modern times who have believed in healing prayer have almost universally prayed prayers of petition for healing. This is partly because prayers of petition are an important and valid way to pray, as for instance, for a new job, and we are most accustomed to it. But to repeat, it is *not* the New Testament pattern for healing prayer (or exorcism).

But now let me say a few things about the Hunters themselves.[3] Charles (1920 - 2010) and Frances (1916 - 2009) were a graced and humble couple. In spite of the large revenues generated by their books and tapes, they collected only a modest salary from their ministry organization (the Billy Graham pattern). They donated the rest of their royalties back into their healing and evangelism ministry. Scandal never touched their ministry.

Charles and Frances met and married late in their lives, in 1970. Charles had been a believer all of his life, but in a cessationist denomination. He and his first wife, Jeanne, had read Agnes Sanford's *Healing Light* and Genevieve Parkhurst's *Healing and Wholeness Are Yours*.[4] Through those books Charles and Jeanne had come to reject cessationism and believed in healing prayer for this day. Mrs. Jeanne Hunter came down with ovarian cancer, and in seeking prayer support for her healing, Charles contacted Mrs. Parkhurst. She came to visit and to pray with Jeanne. The hospital room where Jeanne lay seemed filled with the glory of God, and Jeanne

---

[3] Other than *Charisma* magazine, the Christian press has ignored the Hunters. A Google search gives their website and hits on where to buy their books, plus some ignorant anti-cult sites – the web is full of them. A search in the Christian academic literature shows no hits. The *Charisma* articles are: Bill Shepson's, "Still Happy After All These Years," *Charisma* (August 2000) 95, and E.S Caldwell's, "It is the Hour to Believe," *Charisma & Christian Life*, (October, 1987).

[4] Agnes Sanford, *The Healing Light* (St. Paul: Macalester Park, 1947), Genevieve Parkhurst, *Healing and Wholeness Are Yours* (St. Paul: Macalester Park, 1957).

rallied. During this period, she received a deep inner healing. But ultimately she passed away, happy to go to her Lord.[5] Charles grieved his wife's loss, but he knew that she had gone to her true home, and renewed his own ministry of evangelization.

Frances had been a widow for many years, and became a born-again Christian relatively late in life, when she was forty-nine. At that point she became a self-described "Gospel fanatic" and joined an Evangelical church. She learned soul-wining through Campus Crusade for Christ. Frances discovered she had a special anointing in this and practiced it whenever and however she could. She wrote about her efforts in her first book, *God is Fabulous*.[6]

She also learned about the Holy Spirit. Although her church was not charismatic or Pentecostal, Frances began reading some of the charismatic books just coming to print. On one of her evangelistic tours to Houston, Frances was introduced by a local pastor to Charles Hunter. The couple began corresponding, and within a few months were married. Soon after, they began ministering together. But now, not only proclaiming salvation, but the message of Pentecost and healing.

From the very start of their ministry the Hunters observed and learned healing techniques from a multitude of sources. They picked up the long-standing Pentecostal technique of praying for a person's backache by "leg extension." That is, having the person sit in a chair and praying that the legs be equalized in length. As the legs equalize the spinal column comes into alignment and often this heals the backache. They learned a similar technique, arm extension, from healing evangelist, Joe Poppell. He had been doing it for years to heal upper back pain and chest disorders.

As the Hunters ministered they experienced many miraculous healings. But not to the degree that they expected, and saw described in the Bible, where all who came to Jesus were healed. (Matt 8:16).[7] They asked the Lord for a breakthrough. Charles described what happened:

> One night a man came on the stage, held up by two people, and leaning heavily on two walking canes. He did not have the strength to lift his feet off the floor; he scooted them along…When we finished praying, instead of saying "Praise the Lord and go on your way," we said, "PICK UP YOUR CANES AND WALK!" He lifted his canes off the floor and slid

---

[5] The story of her sickness and death is told in Charles Hunter's, *A Tribute to God* (Kingswood: Hunter Ministries, 2008) Mrs. Parkhurst's ministry to Jeanne is found on pp. 17-43.

[6] Frances Gardner Hunter, *God is Fabulous: The Story of an "Unsaved Christian"* (New York: Family Library, 1973).

[7] It should be noted that in Jesus' own hometown, Nazareth, his healing powers were limited by lack of faith in the population (Matt 13:58).

his feet forward, and he didn't fall! Pretty soon I was running alongside of him across the stage, and he began to say, Praise the Lord![8]

Now, what makes this moment significant is not that it was an original discovery, which it was not. Such commands have been recorded in the lives of the saints and heroes of the Church.[9] For example, spoken healing commands were common in the ministry of the famous faith teacher and healer, Smith Wigglesworth (1859-1947). In one of his several resuscitations from the dead he came into a sick room as a woman died:

> ...I reached over into the bed and pulled her out. I carried her across the room, stood her against the wall and held her up, as she was absolutely dead. I looked into her face and said, "In the name of Jesus I rebuke this death." Her whole body began to tremble. "In the name of Jesus, I command you to walk," I said. I repeated, "In the name of Jesus, walk!" and she walked.[10]

The Hunters' great innovation and gift to Christendom was that thereafter they did it consistently, and taught command healing as the *prerogative of every believer*. It was not just those especially gifted with faith such as Smith Wigglesworth.

At the beginning they believed that it was necessary to *shout* healing commands. My sister, a Catholic nun, who was among the first in her religious order to become a charismatic, recalls a healing event that the Hunters did in her parish in Scarsdale, New York (about 1976). A large Catholic charismatic group came, over four hundred people, and although some healings were done, most persons were entirely put off by the Hunter's shouts and commands. The Hunters soon discerned that the authority of the command did not depend on its decibel level.

In spite of some missteps, the Hunters learned quickly and adjusted. For instance, in order to focus the force of the command (and healing energies), they began asking the supplicant "What does the doctor say about your situation?" This proved to be very helpful in understanding exactly what was wrong and what organ was afflicted. Through trial and error, and consultation with medical professionals, they developed patterns of command prayers for specific diseases. For example, in praying for a person

---

[8] Hunter, *Heal the Sick*, 45-46

[9] Agnes Sanford in her classic work, *The Healing Light* (1947) gave an example of command healing in her own life, but does not make it a major point., and can be easily missed (p.77)

[10] Stanley Howard Frodsham, *Smith Wigglesworth: Apostle of Faith*, (Springfield: Gospel Publishing House, 1990) 59. Originally published in 1948.

with diabetes they would cast out any spirit of inheritance, then command a new pancreas to be formed "in the name of Jesus."[11]

In 1981 the Hunters published their now classic work, *How to Heal the Sick*. This book incorporated a quasi-chiropractic understanding of healing ministry. That is, they had learned from chiropractic physicians, and from observing the results of the arm and leg extensions, that straightening the spine and bringing it to normality was an effective part in healing all sorts of ailments. This is basic to chiropractic theory and practice. They added two other forms of the laying on of hands, one to the neck and another to the pelvis. All of these were combined with commands for healing.

A renowned chiropractor, Dr. Roy Le Roy, heard about the Hunter's ministry and came to witness one of their events with the specific intention of exposing and debunking them. He was astounded at what he saw, and became instead their close friend and ministry adviser.[12] He produced videos and wrote a book to support the Hunter discoveries in healing.

We should make it clear, that the Hunter method and books *do not teach chiropractic manipulation*. Rather they teach the laying on of hands in conjunction with command prayer - and the Holy Spirit does the spine adjustments and other creative miracles.[13]

The Hunters were right about insisting that all Christians should lay hands on the sick. Their book, *If Charles and Frances Can Do It, You Can Do It Too!* says it again and again.[14] What they do not mention is that indeed there are persons with unusual gifts of healing, including themselves. Frances had, for instance, a special anointing to heal cancer – a difficult disease to tackle. Proclaiming that any Christian can minister healing prayer as well as they is an encouragement to others, but also an exaggeration. Few people have the level of anointing they had.

The Hunters continued to search out and test for any new scrap of information that may help in the healing ministry, till the day they went to be with the Lord. They had a panel of medical doctors and chiropractors who advised them and kept them posted on new medical discoveries. For instance, in recent years medical investigators have discovered that human cells give out faint electrical pulses, but that cancer cells give out sig-

---

[11]Hunter, *Handbook of Healing*, 114.

[12]Dr. Roy J. Le Roy, and Norma Jean Le Roy, *The Supernatural Spine* (Kingwood: Hunter Books, 1993).

[13]For example, see the chiropractic charts in the Hunter's book, *If Charles and Frances Can Do It, You Can Do It!* (Kingswood: Hunter Publications, 1997), 44, 92-93.

[14]Ibid. 92.

nificantly different and disharmonious frequencies.[15] With this information the Hunters developed this specific anti-cancer prayer to be prayed over all cancer victims:

> "Devil, I bind you right now by the Spirit of God in Jesus' name. You foul spirit of cancer, I command you to come out right now in the name of Jesus. ...We speak a new immune system into you and we also speak a new blood system so that the cancer cannot spread any further. We command all of the electrical and chemical frequencies in every cell in your body to be in harmony and in balance and digest the bad cells in Jesus' name."[16]

To be clear, this prayer is not a general cure for cancer. I have prayed it over multiple cancer patients without notable effect. It may be that the Hunters were confusing their own special anointing over cancer with the effectiveness of this prayer. But their effort to integrate new medical findings with specific prayers is noteworthy and something that Christians in the healing ministry should follow. In fact, one of the reasons for the great success of the Hunter's healing methods and career is that they have operated in the Biblically mandated mode of "testing discernment." Paul wrote to the Thessalonians: "Do not put out the Spirit's fire; do not treat prophecies with contempt. Test everything. Hold on to the good. Avoid every kind of evil." (1Thess 5:19-21)

Paul wrote with the assumption of the continuous presence and activity of the Holy Spirit in the Church - and also the continuous presence of harassment and confusion caused by demonic spirits.[17] The theology of cessationism was far into the future and probably unimaginable to him. But Paul made it clear that Christians needed the tool of discernment/testing to separate what is good and is from the Holy Spirit, from what is fluff, false or destructive – either "flesh" or demonic. Although the context of Paul's directions in 1 Thess 5 is the prophetic ministry, it is plain that what Paul meant by "test everything" was precisely that, to test every kind of spiritual activity, phenomenon, or manner of spirituality.

With the arrival of heavily doctrinal Christianity, and later with cessationism, the mandate to test was rendered incomprehensible, and in effect

---

[15]On the body's electrical mechanisms see, Robert O Becker, M.D., and Gary Selden, *The Body Electric: Electromagnetism and the Foundation of Life* (New York; William Morrow, 1985). On the electromagnetic properties of cancer cells see the internet article by Steve Haltiwanger, M.D. C.C.N., "The Electrical Properties of Cancer Cells," at http://www.sanum-per-aquam.de/pdfs/spa-study-alkaline-14.pdf.

[16]From the Hunter's website: http://www.cfhunter.org/Prayer_Cancer.htm. Sourced in 2012, but no longer available. Because of complaints that it did not work?

[17]James Kallas, *The Satanward View: A Study of Pauline Theology* (Philadelphia: Westminster Press, 1956), is especially good on this latter point.

became a "historic" passage like 1 Cor 12, to be filed away as interesting but with no present application. The traditional churches, Catholic, Protestant, Eastern or Oriental Orthodox, believed they had it totally right, doctrinally and in practice - so what was there to test?

The ministry of Charles and Frances Hunter has been a golden example of testing discernment. They rediscovered the power of "command healing" and compared it to the biblical text for verification. They tested the utility of combining chiropractic understanding as part of healing prayer and found that it gave good fruit, even though it was not specifically mentioned in the Bible.

The Hunter method, command healing with the chiropractic insights, special leg and arm extensions, etc., has particular significance for the ministry of the PPS. First, it is quicker than petition healing, and often produces results that can be immediately felt by the supplicant, as in the case cited of the girl with the broken ankle (above). This is especially significant in ministering to Nones, who normally would be quick to dismiss healing prayer as "nice poetry but ineffective," or a feel-good psychological event. Second, many people who seem to be OK, actually walk around with back problems, from minor to serious. Using the Hunter method gives immediate and accountable healing to many of these back problems. The people are amazed by the immediate relief, and for many it may be the first time that they have received a recognizable healing from any Christian or church group. Third, if a rapid healing is done to an unbeliever, such healings are a portal to immediate evangelization, and a "decision for Christ" may follow right there. The healing takes the place of the introductory tract or evangelical sermon.

Carolyn and I began to use some of the Hunter arm and leg extensions and command prayers at St. Patrick's as part of the normal healing ministry, that took place right after Holy Communion. We taught some of it to the OSL group. The rector, Fr Gray, noticed it, but did not like it. He called me into his office and told me command healings were part of the folly of the new "name it, claim it heresy" of the "Tulsa folks" (i.e., the "Faith" ministers, Kenneth Hagin, Kenneth Copeland, etc.). He would not be swayed by the scriptures I showed him and forbade us to do it at his church.

That saddened me and I *tried* to be obedient. Wouldn't you know, a few Sundays later Carolyn and I were again on prayer team duty, and a person came to us with a terrible back ache – just the thing the Hunter method does best. I fudged, and healed the man via the "arm extension" – just as the rector glanced over at us.

At this time, I also became enthusiastic about the possibilities of healing homosexual behavior via inner healing. The classic book on this had just come out, Leanne Payne's *The Broken Image*.[18] The rector strongly disagreed with this also, and advocated the liberal view, now a commonly accepted view even among many Bible-believing Christians, that homosexuality is not curable and should not be a healing ministry issue.[19] Principally on this dispute, Carolyn and I were finessed out of the church leadership circle and replaced by a more liberal minded person to lead the Sunday healing teams. The wonderful OSL group was sidelined.

Carolyn and I were saddened and hurt by this. We sought another church home and landed at St. Jude' of Marietta, a really great church where we stayed for over a decade. The rector there, Fr. Frank Baltz, was Bible-believing and totally orthodox.[20] He had no problem with either Lean Payne's work or the Hunter method.

But even at St. Jude's we found resistance to the command mode of healing prayer (this was 1989). Fr. Baltz invited me to lead one of the home Bible study groups of the church. The host of the home found the Hunter method "presumptuous and offensive," and broke up the group rather than have us pray in that way at her home. Unfortunately, there was no OSL group at St. Jude's and so I postponed restarting the PPS ministry.

Shortly after, Fr. Frank asked me to lead a Spanish language service for the Mexicans and El Salvadorians streaming into the area. I did so as lay preacher and healing evangelist. Later, in 2000, I was ordained an Anglican priest. Again, I postponed organizing a prayer station ministry until I could train my Hispanics to do healing prayer and intercession (see below).

All of this happened decades ago. In recent years the command method of healing prayer has percolated through many churches and is more widely accepted, though some more conservative groups still oppose it as heresy, and the web is full of ignorant Christian anti-cult sites that lambaste the Hunters and their teachings.

But now let me back up to the time, 1986, when the OSL group from St. Patrick's went out on the first PPS event.

---

[18]Leanne Payne, *The Broken Image* (Grand Rapids: Cornerstone Books, 1981).

[19]He later wrote a book from this viewpoint, Gray Temple, *Gay Unions: In the Light of Scripture, Tradition and Reason* (New York: Church Publishing, 2000).

[20]His master's thesis at seminary was on Agnes Sanfordd. It stressed her link to the Anglican tradition of healing prayer. Baltz, Frances B. "Agnes Sanford: A Creative Intercessor." MA thesis, Nashotah House, 1979.

# 3

# The public prayer station at Little Five Points

The spot we chose for our first prayer station at Little Five Points was at a renovated ally way at the convergence of Euclid and Moreland Avenues. A small triangular park, called Findey Plaza was about 200 feet just south of the ally way. On some Saturdays, we would vary the PPS position between the park and the ally way, depending on the pedestrian traffic. Most of the time we posted at the ally way, just a bit south of a Pizza joint. There was a concrete park bench at the ally way and a shady tree (neither are there now).

That first Saturday we came with only the prayer station sign and styrofoam ice chest full of soft drinks. Our contact policeman told us it would be OK to bring some folding chairs, and we did that on subsequent outings. Normally, after 6:00pm we put away the PPS sign, and sometimes stepped into the pizza shop and celebrated with a large pizza. We wanted the pizza people not to think we would hurt their business, and we all liked pizza.

At Little Five Points I could use my newly learned Hunter method without guilt. Fr. Gray had instructed me not to use it in church, so here we were at a downtown sidewalk park, surely not a church. That summer I used the Hunter method dozens of times for various diseases and disorders, and not a few back problems. But we did every sort of prayer and prayer counseling too. For example, a well-dressed African-American woman in her late 30s, came up to the Prayer Station for prayer. Her request was for the healing of an upset stomach. Carolyn gently laid hands on her stomach as we both prayed for her complete healing. and she felt immediate relief.

Angela (not her real name) then shared her deeper need. The stomach upset was a sign of a deeper problem, her separation and alienation from her husband. They were together at Little Five points on a "date" to see if there was a path to reconciliation instead of divorce. Carolyn, who worked as a full-time church counselor, took the lead on this case. She asked her various pertinent questions about the state of the marriage, before we began praying for the restoration of her marriage and God's grace to bring forgiveness to both. I mostly prayed silently with an occasional murmured "Amen."

Angela left us thanking us profusely, and with a countenance of joy. As she walked down the sidewalk her husband stepped out of one of the shops and she took hold of his hand. He seemed surprised, but smiled and they continued on their way. We trusted that God's grace would continue to heal that marriage.

That is not to say that professional counselors are necessary at a prayer station, but rather that the Holy Spirit choreographs the needs of the supplicants with the most appropriate prayer counselor. That point came home to me several years earlier when Carolyn and I were serving as volunteers at Mt. Paran's prayer telephone line. We seemed to receive just the right caller, as if some unseen telephone operator was directing the phones. Indeed there was – the Holy Spirit. For instance, one night I was the only male among five prayer counselors on duty. I received a call from a high school girl who was getting pressure from the boyfriend to have sex with him, or else he would dump her. She really liked him. I counseled to hold her ground and her virginity. He would ultimately both respect and truly love her for it. If he kept insisting, I told her, it would be time for her to dump him, and trust that the Lord would bring her the right Christian boyfriend.

But back to a case at the PPS. Carolyn and I were seated on the folding chairs sipping drinks while the station was manned by Liz and her prayer team partner. We watched a young woman come up to the station. The supplicant talked for a minute or so, and then Liz led her to the nearby park bench and motioned us to relieve her at the PPS.

As it turned out, the young lady was considering an abortion for an unplanned pregnancy. Liz was a public-school counselor and had much experience with this issue. Liz counseled her, prayed with her, and gave her specific names and addresses of Christian institutions that would help her bring the baby to term and adopted, if she desired. Liz stayed with her for an hour, before the young lady left quite content.

Not everyone who came to the PPS had a sincere request. On one occasion a young man tried to embarrass us with his prayer request. When we asked what he wanted us to pray for he said, "I want to have some great sex." I suppose he thought we were Puritans as popularly conceived. (The real Puritans had in fact a sound theology of Christian sexuality.) In any case, I did not lose my cool. I prayed, "Oh Father, this young man wants great sex, as most of us do, and I ask in Jesus' name that this be granted in his life, as he finds the beautiful young woman you have set apart to be his mate. May they grow in mutual self-giving, and come to understand that married sex is a symbol of the love Jesus has for those who are in the Church. And grant them children who will grow up in your service. Amen." Carolyn, who initially rolled her eyes at the young man's request, added a hearty "Amen." He walked off a bit chagrinned, but thanked us. Susan, one of the OSL intercessors who was at the PPS from the very beginning, had a similar case. A young man came to the prayer station and his request was to "make a lot of money." Susan's prayer partner on the PPS began to object, "That is not something God answers directly." But Susan disagreed and said. "No, God can answer that prayer." And she prayed, "Lord greatly prosper this young man, and as you do let him grow in relationship with you, and express that in generosity to others." The young man left satisfied. The general point is that practically every desire has a legitimate expression, and the prayer intercessor should recognize that, and pray for the proper good of that desire.

Susan was and continues to this day to be a great prayer intercessor. She had a way at the PPS of praying for the person's expressed request, but after they left, she would pray for a deeper, spiritual need of the person, and continue to do so in her prayer closet at home. From her personal journal of October 1987, two entries:

> Man, 29 years old. Left home at 14. Dresses as a hippy, a remnant from the 1960s…Has saving knowledge of Jesus Christ and amazing spiritual insight. However, he is basically a vagrant, spending his life following the "Grateful Dead," making his home with the Devil, and not for Jesus.
>
> Lord, call T**** to righteousness.
>
> A man in his 20s, long hair in a tail, he stutters. I believe he is a Christian. …He has no car, seems to try out all kinds of churches, but does not stay. Has been attending the "First Existential Church." He thinks he is an intellectual. Lord, clarify B**** thoughts and cleanse him.[1]

At our PPS we periodically prayed for Muslims and other persons who are non-Christian. I found it was important to interact in a respectful manner towards their faith and yet be *subtly* evangelical. I made it a practice

---

[1] Used with Susan's permission. Journal page in author's possession.

to listen to their request and then explain that I pray to God in Jesus' name because that is what we do as Christians. If they were Muslims with a healing need I reminded them that the Koran declares that Jesus is a great healer, and proceed as usual with the laying on of hands, arm extension, etc. I also found that both Sieks and Hindus are very open to receiving healing prayer, as they are generally respectful of Christianity, and understand something about our faith, as there is a significant Christian minority in India.

I had one particularly interesting case. After I had prayed with a Muslim middle aged man with a back pain that was healed (arm and leg extensions) we chatted for a few minutes. He shared his enthusiasm for Islam and the Koran. I said. "You know, the great distinction between the Koran and the Bible is that the Koran knows Jesus as a great prophet and healer, but our Bible goes further, and calls him son of God, and says he arose from the dead. Now we both believe in God as our Father right?"

He answered, "Yes of course."

"Well then, let us right here, in front of God, ask in prayer to make clear to us if Jesus is the son of God, or just a prophet. And we promise to accept God's prompting and guidance on this. OK?" Why yes, that is good." He answered.

"OK, let us see what happens." He left quite content. I still believe that Jesus is the son of God. I trust our agreement prayer was answered.

By late November the weather in Atlanta turned cold, and we suspended the prayer station till the next spring. I recall when we set up again in the spring, the manager of the pizza place saw us coming and shouted with joy, "Your back!" And went into his shop saying, "The prayer station is back, the prayer station is back!" I hadn't been aware that we had specifically prayed for him or any of his waiters, but that must have been the case. There were about a dozen or so prayer intercessors who serviced the PPS, and some must have ministered to the pizza staff on several occasion.

When we began the PPS I had several expectations and hopes. I hoped that we would minister and perhaps convert many persons who were into the metaphysical movement and the occult in that area. Also, that we would give a touch of healing prayer to Christians who were in churches that did not believe in the present reality of healing prayer (cessationists) or that came from churches with poor understanding of healing prayer. The latter did take place often, but we did not have an opportunity to pray for any of the local metaphysical folks. The occult and metaphysical folks simply avoided us, a pattern that held for the two years we ministered at Little Five Points.

I now appreciate more than ever that the PPS is a wonderful way of reaching fallen away Christians, as well as those who were agnostic or "Nones." When we began the PPS in 1987 no one knew that the Church was at the cusp of an era of declining membership and Christian adherence. The moniker "Nones," signifying persons who no longer went to church nor identified themselves as Christian or any other religion, had not been coined. I now see the potential of the PPS as a powerful tool for the Christian churches to reverse the Nones' expansion by demonstrating the power of Jesus' name to heal; and also to bring immediate and powerful prayer to those who have no intention or inclination of going to church.

From the time that the altar call was developed, roughly a hundred years ago, Protestant churches had largely depended on church revivals (really evangelistic campaigns) for the unchurched to make their first commitment to the Lord and enter a local church. The Billy Graham crusades were the gold standard of this approach.[2] They were effective because many Christians could beg and pester their unsaved neighbors and relatives to attend such services. But in the present decade such an approach has become less effective. The Nones and unchurched have no interest in going to any church for a revival of any kind or any time, period. Pestering will only provoke resentment. In fact, many Nones are turning to the occult again, in a revival of the dark side that is reminiscent of the 1970s.[3]

The PPS can do an end run on this situation. It is something that can demonstrate to the Nones and the unchurched the power and reality of God's healing graces, and give them a concrete reason to enter into Christian fellowship. Recently, a nuanced analysis of the Nones appeared which shows that many Nones often drift in and out of various degrees of faith and church participation, depending on mood and personal circumstances. These Nones are termed "liminals." For the Christian evangelist this is a

---

[2] I discuss the "altar call" as a new, Holy Spirit inspired, sacrament in my work, *Forgotten Power: The Significance of the Lord's Supper in Revival* (Grand Rapids: Zondervan, 2003) chapter 12. "From Camp Meeting to Altar Call." A book length history of the altar call is much needed. For an outline of the process see Bill J. Leonard's "Getting Saved in America: Conversion Event in a Pluralistic Culture," *Review and Expositor 82* (Winter 1985) 111-127, and William Oscar Thompson, Jr., "The Public Invitation as a Method of Evangelism: Its Origins and Development," Dissertation: Southwestern Baptist Theological Seminary: Fort Worth, 1979.

[3] Kari Paul, "Why millennials are ditching religion for witchcraft and astrology,' *Market Watch*. Posted Oct. 23, 2017. https://www.marketwatch.com/story/why-millennials-are-ditching-religion-for-witchcraft-and-astrology-2017-10-20.

very useful distinction, for it indicates that many Nones can be more readily evangelized than previously suspected. We found this so at our PPS.[4]

An interview article published recently in *Christianity Today*, the banner American magazine of Evangelicalism, revealed something even more pertinent to the process of ministering to and converting the Nones. It is that they generally mistrust and dislike traditional theological terms such as atonement, sin and repentance (which to them means guilt). Thus communicating the Gospel to them is difficult for most Christians who usually explain it with these terms. But the Nones *do not* react negatively to prayer, which they recognize as active in all religions. Thus praying with a none can be an effective first encounter with such a person.[5] This is precisely what a PPS intercessor can do well.

But let me finish this chapter by pointing out that there are still many churches which are cessationist, or near cessationist. Just recently (summer of 2017) I was called to do a teaching and healing mission at a camp meeting in Pennsylvania. It was a region of highly conservative, lovely and devote Believers, many from Amish or Brethren background. As I taught about the laying on of hands and urged several prayer exercises on the audience, some persons walked out in a huff. Praying for healing with the laying on of hands would not fit their cessationist theology.

Thankfully, many in the audience were open to this teaching and several wonderful miracles of healing occurred as they laid hands on one another for healing. One man in his mid-thirties came up to me as I was packing up to go home. He said, "I have been in church for over three years and no one ever offered to pray for my healing needs. I received a healing today, thank you." We should be way beyond that sort of thing, but we are not. A PPS team can minister to that type of Christian and enlighten reluctant and stubborn pastors that healing is real, and for this age, and they better attend to it.

We stopped the PPS in mid-summer of 1989 in rather sad circumstances. The TV-Evangelist scandals involving Jim Baaker and his wife Tammy, and the Jimmy Swaggert sex scandal had broken out. We found that the public was now highly cynical and mostly refused prayer. If the leaders were corrupt, who could trust us? I felt as the OSL convener that I could not expect our wonderful prayer team to continue to give up their

---

[4]Bradley Wright, "20% of Americans are in the Threshold of Religion," *Christianity Today*. Posted September 20, 2017. http://www.christianitytoday.com/edstetzer/2017/september/20-of-americans-are-on-threshold-of-religion.html

[5]Binder, Melissa, "Evangelism is Alive and Well in Portland: How Pastors, Evangelists, and Residents are Sharing the Good News among the City's "Nones" and Muslim Refugees," *Christianity Today* (61 no 3 Apr 2017) 36-38, 40.

Saturday afternoons, which was normally family time, just to pray for one or two persons. We decided to let some time pass before we ventured out again. But that never happened with the St. Patrick's OSL.

# 4

# Public prayer stations on the run

When I was Hispanic pastor at St. Jude's I made every effort to model and teach the healing ministry to my congregation. In fact, just a few months after I was given that charge I led the first Spanish workshop on healing in our church. This was a compression of the eight week course I had originally learned from the Burnetts (see above) into a single four-hour program. It was very successful, helped by the availability of the Spanish translation of *How to Heal the sick*, which was mandatory for the course.[1] I presented that workshop periodically in the course of my tenure at St. Jude's, and later as Hispanic pastor at Light of Christ (Anglican).

The latter church was a "remnant" congregation formed out of St. Jude's parishioners, Anglos and Hispanics, who decided to leave St. Jude's after Fr. Gene Robinson, a practicing homosexual, was ordained bishop in the Episcopal Church. Many other congregations all over the nation also split at this time. Our Hispanic section at Light of Christ was called "San Lazaro" after Lazarus the leper. He is famous in Hispanic countries as a Saint to pray to for impossible or near hopeless situations.

Finding and moving into a new building, getting enough chairs, etc., were all time consuming, but we finally managed to field several PPS outings. Our prayer team from San Lazaro first tried a PPS at a nearby strip mall that catered to Hispanics. We did it for two Saturdays with relatively merger results. The lesson was that a strip mall in not really a pedestrian

---

[1] Charles Hunter, and Frances Hunter, *Como Sanar los Enfermos* (Houston: Hunter Books, 1988).

walk-way. That is, people park in front of the businesses they go to, but do not walk the strip, as in a mall. The second Saturday I brought a bullhorn to broadcast our ministry. It was still hard to get people to come, although the few that did were well serviced by our effective prayer team. Again, it was really unfair to ask my prayer team to lose half their Saturday (family time) to pray for just a few people. So the strip mall ministry was cancelled.

Incidentally, I have never found a mall owner that would allow a PPS on their premises in spite of much trying. It would be wonderful if Christian mall owners allowed it. In one case a PPS was allowed in a mall. It was from the "Prayer Stop" ministry (see below) whose founder was a very successful businessman and was able to use his business and social connections to do so.

We brain-stormed about where to go next, and someone suggested one of the local flea markets. I scouted that idea out, but was rebuffed repeatedly. The owners gave us one excuse or another, as in, if they allow our church to do it, every single church in town will want space also. But finally, I found a flea market some dozen miles or so away that let us have a booth.

We did three Saturday prayer station events. I was as proud as could be seeing my Hispanic team do effective healing and intercessory prayers. I had the luxury of taking breaks and strolling along the booths to see what junk I might be interested in, and knew the intercessors would do well without my presence. But the local fire marshal who inspected the area determined that the flea market was set up over a former landfill, and the garbage underneath was breaking down into methane and leaking to the surface. An explosion could result, and the site was shut down. Score another one for Ol'Scratch.

That was the last attempt at a Hispanic prayer station at San Lazaro. It was not, however, the last prayer station event I did at Light of Christ. There I was also the chaplain of an OSL group that was mostly Anglo, and came from a variety of Episcopal, Anglican and Methodist churches in the area. We met monthly to discuss and practice healing prayer. The group always had friends or relatives who were ill and brought in for prayer – it was a wonderful OSL chapter.

I talked about the prayer station, and a group of six volunteered to try one. This event took place during a music festival at Marietta square (Glover Park) at the center of the old Marietta. This is a lovely section of boutique businesses and restaurants. The organizers of the festival would not allow us a booth for the usual reasons. However, I managed to get a parade permit from city hall for the same day and next to the most trafficked entrance to the square. There is no such thing as a "prayer station permit," so a parade permit had to do, even though we did not go anywhere.

It was wonderful and effective. Our station was less than fifteen feet from a traffic light right at the corner. There was a bench nearby, and there was plenty of pedestrian traffic going in and out. It was very hot that day, so the intercessors crew took turns on station, and at the delicatesen just across the street, enjoying drinks and snacks.

One of the intercessors had a brilliant idea. She got a large poster sheet that some vendor had just discarded, and wrote on the back in large letters, "Drive-by Prayer." She held up the sign when the cars were stopped at the red light she asked if anyone wanted a quick prayer for any intention. Surprisingly, many said yes, and several persons drove around a second time for more prayer. One person did that, then parked his car and came to the station for further prayer. The drive-by prayers were all done with some humor, but with sincerity and were very effective. It was a joy to watch. I am really sorry we don't have a picture of this.

At the PPS a man in his early 40s and looking in the prime of health, walked up for prayer. He had a serious back problem with a herniated vertebra and going into surgery soon. He was in pain all the time. I ministered to him with the usual arm and leg extension commands, "In Jesus's name, left leg extend..." etc. After five minutes of ministry he was completely pain free and totally astounded. He was a Christian but had never been in a church that "prayed like this," and, where could he go to bring his friends. That question saddened me, as the pastor of Light of Christ, although charismatic, had at the same time serious unresolved spiritual faults which was affecting the church and making my stay at Light of Christ uncomfortable. All I could say was, "Find a good Spirit-filled church, perhaps a Vineyard church near you."

In fact, within six months of that prayer station event the rector had managed to make plain that the Hispanics were of little consideration, and my congregation dwindled to a prayer group of less than a dozen people.[2] I closed it down and felt that the Lord wanted me to focus on writing, and left that church. What I did not know was that the rector, in his animus toward me, also made the OSL group unwelcome, and we had to find new quarters. We never did find a satisfactory alternative.[3] After this, Carolyn and I ministered at several Pentecostal churches as healing coordinators.

---

[2]No need to go into the details of this sad situation. The pastor died of cancer several years later.

[3]Here I must admit that I blundered seriously. As chaplain I should have stayed in the background, but I slowly assumed leadership, to the offense of the elected conveners

34  The Public Prayer Station

Carolyn was also full time counselor at these churches. We did a wonderful PPS event at one of these, Faith Point Church, in conjunction with two other churches, El Forro (Hispanic) and Dayspring Church (Pentecostal), all from the area, Canton, Georgia, where we lived.

What we did there may be a useful model for many Christian groups. The location was an apartment complex designed for low income women and their children. Many of those living there came out of abusive relationships, and the community is gated for their protection. It also includes offices for support groups, counseling and job training NGOs.

The event was a church "love fest". Faith Point brought in a food wagon and served free hot dogs and chips. Dayspring provided the tent set-up and the preaching and some music. El Forro, provided a choir.

The Faith Point "chuck wagon" with pastors Ronny and Seth in charge of not burning the franks, and the musicians from El Foro Church

The love fest was a terrific success. Several persons made their first commitment to the Lord, and we prayed over a dozen people for varied needs. These included two serious illnesses, one a case of ALS and another a lung problem - as in needing a lung transplant. We also prayed for a bevy of less dramatic, but necessary needs, as for better employment, new spouse, etc.

We also had the experience of a sudden addition to the PPS intercessors that I had not planned on. In the afternoon there was a slow period and I was alone at the PPS. A young African-American man from Dayspring Church came up and asked if he could pray for the people with us. He had noticed what we were doing and liked the idea. Normally I would have politely refused the offer and explained that this needed special training. But I felt, since I knew he came from a Pentecostal church, that it was OK to let him try. I would be there in case he started to bungle the job.

At the PPS with the prophetic intercessor from Dayspring Church. Local folks in the foreground

No such thing happened. The young man, in fact, had the gift of prophecy and prayer, as he prayed for the supplicant's request, he also interjected prophetic affirmations, and encouragement (1 Cor 12: 3-4). I could sense they were right on the mark. It was an awesome experience for me, and for the rest of the afternoon I hardly said a word, except an occasional "Amen" to his prayers and prophetic utterances.

This brings up a serious issue about the role of the gifts of the Spirit at the PPS. Should such gifts be used on a regular basis? Certainly healing prayer is a constant, and in a certain sense healing is one of the gifts of the Spirit (1 Cor 12: 9). But healing is more an "authority" gift of all Christians and in a sense is "pre-Pentecost." The seventy-two disciples had the gift at the beginning of Jesus' ministry and that was years before Pentecost day. But what of the other gifts of the Spirit, specifically prophecy, and words of wisdom? Some of the passers-by might think that the prophecy utterances are a sign of a delusional mind and be offended rather than edified or comforted.

I believe the answer to this issue is a definite "maybe." That is, there are several factors to consider. In the women's complex where we ministered, many of the persons were from Pentecostal churches, or at least had Pentecostal friends. They mostly had enough knowledge of the gifts of the Spirit so as not to be confused or frightened. But in another community setting it might be better not to use the word gifts. At Little Five Points many of the supplicants were agnostic and suspicious of Christianity in general, and a prophetic utterance and tongues might backfire and confirm in the supplicant's mind that Christians are nuts. Our teams had to be prudent in the public use of the gifts.

Let me also point out that church events as these solve the pedestrian problem of the PPSs. The people come to the event location for food, or music, or because their kids have drifted in, and are ministered to when they see that intercessors are praying for others and step up for their own needs. Many churches do this sort of love feast in low income neighborhoods and trailer parks, and the PPS is a natural fit for these events (see an example below, chapter, 8).

As I write the first draft of this work (September, 2017) the three hurricanes that hit Texas, Florida and Puerto Rico have just passed, and all regions are being serviced and helped by Christian volunteers. The Church has learned to do this well especially after the disaster of hurricane Katrina that hit New Orleans. My thought is that the people in the afflicted areas need prayer support as well a physical and logistical aid. Yes, we can pray long distance prayers, and that is helpful. But the Christian volunteers could also set up PPSs in the devastated areas and give the personal and special touch of the laying on of hands in prayer. Perhaps an ideal church relief group in the future would be made of young healthy adults to help in the physical cleanup work, and older "seasoned citizens" who are experienced in intercessory and healing prayer to man a PPS.

I posted this suggestion on my Facebook page and received a sharp rebuke from someone who had experience on disaster relief events. He affirmed that the PPS would be a nuisance, getting in the way of the debris removal and most probably the police would send it away. I believe he was thinking of the YWAM prayer station, whose set-up includes a large folding table and a large sign (see below). That indeed does take up a chunk of sidewalk room, and may be inappropriate in certain clean-up situations. But it is more likely that a suitable site could be found for it that is both visible to the public, and out of the immediate trash removal area, as in, the concrete slab of a demolished home or car port. In any case, the PPS we have used and suggested has a very small footprint and should present no interference to the work of debris cleanup.

Just a month later (October of 2017) I was invited by the pastor of Floodgate Church, Bill Bolin, in Brighten, Michigan, to help with a yearly conference he holds called "Firefall." He also wanted me to demonstrate a PPS to his church. Bill and his wife, Clara, lead a really great church. It is filled with folks who are enthusiastic about the Lord and fervent in prayer, and well-schooled in healing and intercessory prayer. There was no need for me to go there and do my standard healing workshop. In fact, Joan Hunter had done a healing teaching and prayer event at last year's Firefall.

The group from Floodgate that went out to do the PPS was over 25 persons, including several youths. Pictured below are some of them. Pastor Bill had invited me to bring my original prayer station sign, which is still "serviceable." (That is an Army phase for used and junky equipment that still works OK—note the picture of it in my garage.)

The original PPS sign after 30 years of action. Would you call this "serviceable," or just a piece of junk? Who knows? It may be worth big money in the Antiques Road Show in the future.

The prayer station outing was a great success in spite of the "stony ground" we sowed in. We went to the center of Ann Arbor (about twenty minutes from the church) which is pedestrian friendly and boutique laden, and frequented mostly by students and faculty of the University of Michigan. This is a very secular and "New Age" demographic, and resistant to the Gospel. The response to our invitations to prayer was scant compared to a similar effort in my home state of Georgia where the population is much more Christian. In spite of that, we got one "salvation" of a student who had never given her life to the Lord, and a half dozen significant healings. One was of a homeless veteran who had severe back problems and arthritis all over his back.

Part of the wonderful PPS crew from Floodgate Church
Note the PPS made cheaply and quickly.

The other interesting thing about this outing was that we only had one sign for 25+ people, so many went out on their own in the park area, or nearby eateries, two by two, and sought the Lord's guidance about whom to pray for. That was successful, and several persons received both healing prayer and godly counsel. It was a great crew, and a great day for "people fishing," as the Lord commanded us (Matt 4:19). I urged the volunteers to keep at it in the same spot, as every time they return they deposit a grace over the area that will limit the local demonic "powers" and make each additional outing more fruitful. Note that the PPS ministry based in the UK, called HOTS, urges the same sort of patient repletion of the PPS ministry (see below). Peppering the event with spiritual warfare prayer beforehand would also help.

I don't want to end this section without mentioning an article I ran into. It describes a Lutheran pastor's Thursday mornings at his local coffee shop. He buys a cup of coffee, sits at a table and places a sign on the table that says "free prayer." Instead of a "prayer intercessor" badge or ministry vest, his clerical suit and collar identify him as the prayer intercessor. The table becomes a PPS in a coffee shop. Sometimes his own parishioners come for prayer, but mostly it is strangers who have come for coffee. The link to the article is in the footnote below, and some of the stories are awesome.[4]

---

[4] Thomas Rusert, "Why I offer "Free Prayer" in a Coffee Shop." *Faith and Leadership*. Accessed Sept. 14, 2017. http://www.ministrymatters.com/all/entry/6670/why-i-offer-free-prayer-in-a-coffee-shop

# 5

# Deliverance in the Park

After my entry into the Charismatic Renewal, I developed an interest in the ministry of exorcism. I set a goal to write a book on the different approaches to exorcism and deliverance: Catholic, the Pentecostal/charismatic, and the Protestant. I managed to do much reading and cassette listening in this area, and did several exorcisms as a lay charismatic.[1] This was the Lord's way of showing me the literature I was reading was real. By Divine inspiration (and protection) I put aside that project. I believed I needed more time and spiritual maturity to do it – I was right.[2] But the knowledge I gained in this attempt helped me later on more than one occasion as pastor, and when ministering at PPSs.

About the third or fourth Saturday at the Little Five Points, Carolyn and I were standing by our PPS sign, and two other prayer intercessors were a few yards away on folding chairs we had brought – we wanted to leave the park bench to the locals. A tall, light skinned African American

---

[1] In the Western Church, especially after the Middle Ages, the ministry of exorcism was increasingly restricted to ordained clergy. Pentecostals do not put much credence in ordination as a criterion for the ministry of exorcism, and recognize the ability to cast out demons as a universal Christian characteristic, although certain persons are recognized as especially gifted in this ministry.

[2] There is a recent work that covers the topic of comparative exorcism ministry, but it is marred by a bias against the Pentecostal tradition: James M. Collins', *Exorcism and Deliverance Ministry in the Twentieth Century* (Milton Keynes: Patternoster, 2009). I have not written the book on comparative exorcism yet, but many of my writings deal with the demonic, as for instance this posting: "If it Quacks Like a Duck: The Discovery of the Demonic by Secular Psychiatrists," *Anglican Pentecostal.* Posted June 6, 2017. http://anglicalpentecostal.blogspot.com/2017/06/if-it-quacks-like-duck-discovery-of.html

male in khaki shorts and white shirt passed by and I gave my usual invitation. He stopped and considered for a second, and then stepped up to the prayer station.[3] "Yes, I have a neighbor who is addicted to drugs and it is ruining his life."

Carolyn and I prayed for his neighbor in proxy, by laying hands on Tom (that was not his name). I rebuked the spirit of addiction and asked the Lord to totally set him free. The supplicant was happy with the way we prayed, and went off thanking us. I resumed my invitations to other passersby.

Ten minutes later he returned and confessed that he also had a serious drug problem. That is not an uncommon pattern, as many persons are reluctant to share their most pressing (or embarrassing need) to total strangers. But our prayers had convinced him that we could be trusted. He shared his tragic story. He was an engineer and well on his way to the American Dream. But he became addicted to cocaine, and lost his job and family, and now was on the edge of skid row. He had been a church-going man, but after his wife left him he stopped attending.

We invited him to sit at the nearby bench, and asked if he would let us pray for him by casting out the demons of addiction and anything else in him. He agreed. I motioned the other team members to join us. Carolyn and another team member began praying in tongues. After a few moments, I began, "In Jesus' name I come against any and all evil spirits inhabiting and harassing Tom! I come against the spirit of addiction and I command you OUT!"

Tom shook as if he was struck by some invisible object. Carolyn immediately added, "Spirit of despair." She was functioning with the gift of discernment of spirits (1 Cor 12:10) and I commanded, "In Jesus name, spirit of despair, come out!" Again, Tom shook. Carolyn injected, "Spirit of suicide." I continued, "Spirit of suicide, leave NOW!" Again, Tom quaked. "Any more?" I asked Carolyn? She prayed in tongues for a few seconds, "Spirit of rejection, from childhood."

I continued, "Foul spirit of rejection, leave now in Jesus name!" Tom shook yet again. "More?" I asked. Carolyn answered, "I don't see anything else." I stepped up to Tom and laid my hand on his head. "In Jesus' name, I ask the Holy Spirit to flow into you, and fill every empty space that the demons occupied. I command your neurological system, especially the brain, to be cleansed of all addiction to cocaine or any other drug." As I was pray-

---

[3]This exorcism was briefly described in my original article on the prayer station, "Ministry at Little Five Points," *Acts 29* (May, 1988) 2.

ing this I could feel the vibrating energies of God flowing into Tom. His face came alive with surprise and joy.

A few moments later he got up, declaring, "I feel like a new man. I am completely... free." We prayed for him a little longer, asking the Lord to restore his career and family. I counseled him that he must go back to church, to get Christian fellowship and continued support to rebuff any demonic re-infestation. Tom agreed and walked away thanking us and praising the Lord.

I never heard from Tom again, so I can't affirm that his deliverance stuck, or if he allowed the spirits to come back in and finish the ruination of his life (Matt 12:43-45). But I can affirm that he was delivered that day. This, by the way, is a disadvantage of having a prayer station far from your home church, you cannot invite the person to your church to do follow up discipleship.

That exorcism occurred back in 1987. Since then I have a half dozen others, but always in the setting of a church, and most after I was ordained as an Anglican priest. As I was ready to do the first draft of this chapter I thought I would say that such public exorcisms are imprudent, and the successful case of Tom's exorcism was due to God's grace overcoming my youthful indiscretion. Rather, exorcisms should be done with preparation and care, and at least in private and possibly with medical screening beforehand. In effect, a PPS deliverance should not be done.

But I received a check in my spirit about taking this approach. And I was reminded by the Holy Spirit of the exorcisms in the Gospels. In the New Testament exorcisms were done by Jesus, his Apostles and disciples in public, but with no lengthy preparation. Exorcisms occurred as immediate, unplanned confrontations with the demonic.[4] In fact, in the first ministry campaign Jesus' disciples reported back with great joy that they had healed the sick and cast out demons (Luke 10:17) There was no hint there of special preparations, ministry ordinations, nor of privacy concerns, which have become a modern fetish.[5] Rather, exorcism was an integral part of the healing ministry. In the Gospels, when a person is sick from a disease, hands are laid on and the disease cast out (command mode), but when the sickness or disorder is due to a demon, the demon is cast out. It is all a seamless ministry of restoring wellness.

---

[4] On the important, and lamentably ignored, issue of countering the Kingdom of Satan as one of the chief duties of the Church, see the classic work by James Kallas, *The Stanward View: Studies in Pauline theology*. (Philadelphia, Westminster, 1966).

[5] To be fair, there is one instance where Jesus hints certain types of demons need prayer, and not merely by command (Mk 9:29). This leaves room for the Catholic understanding of substantial preparation.

As you go, preach this message: 'The kingdom of heaven is near.' Heal the sick, raise the dead, cleanse those who have leprosy, drive out demons. Freely you have received, freely give. (Mt 10:6-8)

Similarly, in the early church, exorcism was a lay matter in the hands of those gifted in that ministry. Irenaeus of Lyons, Bishop and writer against heretics wrote:

> "Those who are in truth His disciples, receiving grace from Him, do in His name perform miracles, so as to promote the welfare of other men, according to the gift which each one has received from Him. For some do certainly and truly drive out devils, so that those who have thus been cleansed from evil spirits frequently both believe in Christ and join themselves to the Church . . . others still, heal the sick by laying their hands upon them, and they are made whole.[6]

Our attitude towards exorcism and deliverance ministries, and our ability to accept the plain biblical evidence, is distorted by multiple factors. In the secular West there is a strong prejudice to disbelieve in the reality of the demonic, and reduce demonic manifestations to instances of abnormal psychology.

Sadly, the poverty of Protestant tradition on exorcism produced by the theology of cessationism has left little to say about the topic, leaving a tremendous ignorance gap.[7] This leads many Protestant ministers, especially those influenced by liberal theology, to dismiss demonic activities and manifestations as psychological abnormalities, and more than likely refer the demon infested person to a psychiatrist.[8] Also, the predominance of the Roman Catholic traditions on exorcism, as portrayed in the film "The Exorcist," has sown certain distortions. In fact, it is among the Pentecostals and charismatics that the Protestant wing of Christianity has substantially recovered a robust and biblical practice of exorcism and deliverance as a routine practice.[9]

---

[6] Irenaeus, *Against Heresies.*

[7] I discuss this extensively in *Quenching the Spirit* and *Agnes Sanford and Her Companions*. By the mid-Twentieth Century there was some attention to the demonic by Protestant pastors and theologians – way over-due and mostly ignored by their colleagues.

[8] Collins', *Exorcism and Deliverance Ministry* calls the renewed Protestants understandings of exorcism "evangelical fundamentalist." See his chapter four, "Evangelical Fundamentalist Deliverance Ministry."

[9] The classic Pentecostal text on exorcism and deliverance is the work by Frank and Ida Mae Hammon, *Pigs in the Parlor: A Practical Guide to Deliverance* (Kirkwood: Impact, 1979). Don Basham's *Deliver Us From Evil* (Old Tappen: Chosen, 1972) might be cited as one of many excellent works in the charismatic wing.

Theological confusion about exorcism and deliverance is exacerbated by a raging theological divide, fueled mostly by the non-charismatic Evangelical wing of Protestantism. Certain Evangelicals claim that a Christian cannot possibly be possessed or infected by demonic entities. The constant experience of ministers who actually venture out in this field should put that theory to rest. Cases like Tom, i.e., persons who are Christian but have slid in their spiritual lives, come up frequently.[10] Scripturally, the account of Ananias and Sepphira (Acts 5:1-3) a born-again and Spirit-filled couple in the Jerusalem Jewish/Christian community who let Satan "fill their hearts" is biblical proof enough that at times Christians need deliverance ministry.

A limited recovery of exorcism and deliverance ministry in Protestantism came via Nineteenth Century Protestant missionaries in Asia and Africa. There missionaries encountered societies where the Gospel had never been preached and the demonic presence overt. The most famous instance of this was the work of the Rev. John Nevius, perhaps the most distinguished American missionary in a century filled with heroic and dedicated missionaries. He came to China out of seminary a convinced cessationist, as all his colleagues. He was led by the example of his own converts. They read the Bible simply and without its cessationist overlay, and understood that demons were real, and could be exorcised by the name of Jesus for the healing of their friends and neighbors. This was a general pattern for many missionaries in Asia and Africa. The native lay exorcists not only taught the ministry of exorcism to their Protestant missionary teachers, but also did most of the actual ministry in this area.[11]

That lesson from the 1900s was mostly ignored or rationalized away as pertaining only to non-Christian countries, and therefore unnecessary in Europe and America. It was forgotten until a few evangelical scholars half a century later began a new series of investigation into the occult and demonology.[12] Many mainline ministers, especially in the liberal persuasion still dismiss the matter of the demonic and exorcism as mere "superstition" or misdiagnosed as abnormal psychology.[13]

---

[10] A good presentation from someone experienced in healing and deliverance of this issue is in the blog, "Can a Christian Have a Demon?" *Great Bible Study*. Accessed July 18, 2017. http://www.greatbiblestudy.com/deliverance_believers.php

[11] William De Arteaga, "The Holy Spirit Gives a Lesson in Chinese," *Pneuma Review*. Posted May 10, 2014. http://pneumareview.com/the-rev-john-l-nevius-the-holy-spirit-gives-a-lesson-in-chinese/

[12] Collins, *Exorcism and Deliverance*, chapter four.

[13] A classic of this destructive form of interpreting the demonic is Henry Ansger Kelly's, *The Devil, Demonology and Witchcraft: The Development of Christian Belief in Evil* (Garden City: Doubleday, 1968).

The Catholic tradition has many good points and is especially useful in dealing with persons who are seriously infected by the demonic – possessed. That is, a person's behavior is dominated by a demonic spirit, and may manifest bizarre phenomenon. This was well represented in the movie the "Exorcist," based on the book of the same name, and which in turn was based on a real case.[14] Such total possession is very rare (and very destructive). I personally have never encountered anything that severe, but the literature on such severe possessions is consistent throughout the ages and should not be doubted even if it makes one uncomfortable.

But the Catholic understanding of possession and exorcism, with the priest as lead minister, leaves unanswered and under-ministered the whole issue of lesser spirits and lesser states of demonic infestation. For instance, Tom, the engineer, was not "possessed" in the classic sense, but he had a spirit of addiction and other spirits.[15] The Catholic lack in this area came home to me when I watched the excellent PBS program "The American Experience" on President John Kennedy. As president, and even before, he had repeated trysts and affairs in spite of having a beautiful wife. Kennedy was asked by a friend why he had so many of these, and he answered, "I am compelled to do that…"[16] President Kennedy was not "possessed" in the Catholic definition of the word, but he did need serious deliverance ministry for a spirit of fornication and other attaching spirits. No priest or anyone else ministered to him in that way, and more than likely would have defined Kennedy's situation as needing repentance, confession and the practice of self-control, but not necessarily an issue of demonic influence.[17]

The Episcopal/Anglican tradition (my tradition) has no cannon or written rules as to who can lead in exorcism and deliverance ministry. Signifi-

---

[14]William Peter Blatty, *The Exorcist* (New York: Harper & Row, 1971). A discussion of the original case upon which the novel and movie were based is found in, Howard Newman's, *The Exorcist: The Strange Story Behind the Film* (New York: Pinnacle, 1974).

[15]I believe these lesser sprits to be the "elemental spirits" mentioned by Paul in Gal 4:3 and Col 2:8, and are more "psychic clusters" than demonic entities with intact personalities

[16]PBS, *"JFK" The American Experience* series. Aired Nov. 11, 2013. Access to the entire program is at: http://www.pbs.org/video/2365118698/

[17]t is my opinion that Kennedy's spirit of fornication, and other spirits which laid unmolested by any deliverance ministry, led to his weakness of character. He was not only unfaithful to his wife, but unfaithful to the Cuban heroes at the Bay of Pigs who were defeated for lack of promised American air support. Further, he was unfaithful to the truth. He had campaigned that President Eisenhower (and Nixon) had allowed the Russians to outpace the U.S in ballistic missiles, but when he got to be President he was shown the intelligence data which showed that claim was not true. Rather than face embarrassment, he chose to order 1.000 new intercontinental missiles to "catch up" with the USSR. This ignited the very costly missile, anti-missile, arms race, as the Russians interpreted this as an attempt to build a "first strike" capability

cantly, one of the questions of the Episcopal catechism, found in the *Book of Common Prayer*, is:

Q. Who are the ministers of the Church?

A. The ministers of the Church are lay persons, bishops, priests, and deacons.[18]

Further questions in the catechism reveal that the Bishops and priest administer the sacraments. But the issue of healing prayer, and deliverance/exorcism (which were never defined as sacraments in any Christian church) is left unmentioned.

When I first encountered the Charismatic renewal as a Roman Catholic in the 1970s, our prayer group often worshiped together with an Episcopal group at St. Philips' Cathedral. There the Dean of the Cathedral, and a leader of the charismatics in that church, was the Rev. David Collins. He was prominent in the Episcopal Church as the leader of the Episcopal House of Deputies, a very prestigious and responsible position. Dean Collins was an excellent priest and preacher, but it was his wife Jenny who had the anointing for deliverance and exorcism ministry. Whenever some case presented itself at the Cathedral that might have demonic origins, the person was referred to Jenny.[19] This is not to say that having an ordained, trained and designated clerical exorcist is not useful. In my own denomination there is in fact such a diocesan position, and that person, just like a designated Catholic exorcist, handles the most serious cases of possession.

On the issue of lay exorcism ministry, let me share my favorite story on this. When I was pastor of San Lazaro in Marietta, I taught my congregation the healing ministry using the Hunter materials which includes instruction on deliverance. We demonstrated healing at practically every service as someone or another would invariably have some ailment or bring someone who did. Several in the congregation took this to heart and flowered in that ministry.

On one occasion we had a serious deliverance right in the middle of a service. Demons really do not like intense praise music, and will often act up during its performance.[20] The lady manifesting was one of our regulars,

---

[18] BCP, 1979 "The Catechism."

[19] For the story of the Collins' joint ministry to the charismatic community in Georgia, see Dean David Collins' autobiography, *There is a Lad Here* (Darien: Darien News, 1996). Dean Collins passed to his heavenly reward in 2017, "full of years" – he was a naval officer in World War II.

[20] This is more common in Africa, where witchcraft is prevalent. In fact, some pastors consider a service incomplete and lacking in the Spirit if a demon does not manifest and is thrown out.

and a good Christian. However, she had played with the Ouija Board in her youth, and a demon got in (not a rare occurrence). My assistant priest and several lay persons cast the demon out right then and there as I went on to do Holy Communion – I figured the practical experience of an exorcism is better than any sermon I could give. In fact, the following Sunday I preached about exorcism and answered the congregation's questions about the matter.

Years later, after I had retired from the church, I received a call form Ruben, one of my elders. I could hear chaotic background noises. He said, "Padre Bill, I am at church, but the priest is gone. We have a lady with a demon here; I need your help in casting him out." (More noise and commotion.) "Oh wait, I remember. I will call back." Phone hangs up. Ten minutes later he calls, "I remembered and I cast the demon out. Everything is OK here. Thank you." I answered, "Good job Ruben, blessings to your family." When I hung up I felt God was telling me, "Good job, Bill, you taught them well."

All of which is to say that, in spite of the disdain of this type of ministry by many clergy, and certainly their opposition to lay persons doing anything like this in public, *Tom's exorcism at the park bench was in perfect Biblical order.* Some one in every PPS team should be prepared to address and confront the demonic, or at least have some knowledge on this topic - as in reading some of the basic books on deliverance I am suggesting in the resource section (below).

Sadly, it is still true that many Christians who are mature and experienced in prayer have had very little teaching on the issue of deliverance/exorcism. It is safe to say that in a majority of Protestant seminaries the topic is not taught. I recall a sad instance back in the 1980's when I attended for a season a noted Methodist seminary (and ultimately left, disgusted with its predominantly liberal and even apostate faculty). In a course on missions every student had to present his paper in class. I did a project on the Rev. John Nevius (mentioned above). After my presentation, which included a brief bibliography of useful books on exorcism, the fellow students came to me privately and thanked me for the presentation and bibliography. I remember clearly (though it was almost forty years ago) one telling me, "Thank you, what you gave in class was the only instruction I have received on exorcism in my three years here." I doubt the situation is much changed at that seminary.

# Part II

# Taking the Public Prayer Station to the World

In this section we will look at several ministries that have taken the PPS beyond our pioneer efforts. The YWAM originating PPS, the UK based ministry, Healing on the Streets (HOTS), and the "Prayer Stop" ministry were all founded by evangelists with experience in various forms of street ministry. These ministries dealt with the issue of follow up and further discipleship that our PPS efforts did not tackle. The YWAM based ministry spread its brand of the PPS world-wide via its PPS kits. The HOTS ministry is mostly centered in the UK, but with stations in Europe and Scandinavia, and a few in the United States. HOTS has demonstrated an example of ministering in the power of the Spirit even in areas where the Christian faith is weak, such as Northern Europe. The "Prayer Stop" ministry is the newest player and is based primarily in the United States.

# 6

# YWAM brings the Public Prayer Station to the nations

YWAM (Youth With A Mission) is one of the planet's greatest Evangelical para-church organizations, and out of it came an effective and numerically large PPS ministry. YWAM was founded in 1960 by Loren Cunningham, as a group to train and equip short term missionaries. These missionaries would be focused on specific tasks, such as building churches or repairing roads. YWAM grew from its initial emphasis to include many types of aid and missionary work, though it still focuses on evangelization by word and deed. Especially noteworthy are its hospital equipped "Mercy Ships" which anchor at places where disaster had hit or medical needs are great. YWAM also operates schools for missions and discipleship, and these continue to this day and have a reputation for their effectiveness.

Unlike other large organizations, YWAM has maintained a loose administrative structure. This allows flexibility, and has even permitted some of its components to separate from YWAM. This happened with the Mercy Ships (some of the smaller ones still operate directly under YWAM). YWAM regional directors are allowed great flexibility in how to use their resources and volunteers to meet the needs of advancing the Gospel.

In this regard, in 1992, the director for YWAM in the New York area, Nick Sovaca, sensed that the Lord was telling him to take his group and pray for people in the street. He may, or may not, have earlier run across our article in *Acts 29* (May, 1988) which described the first prayer station. Mr. Sovaca reports that he was directly guided by the Lord to establish a pray station without any other inspiration.[1] That is very possible, or it may be that he ran across an account of our first prayer station and it lodged in his subconscious and he did not remember.

The Holy Spirit has often inspirited persons at different times and locations with the same message. For instance, for decades Pentecostal historians believed that the Azusa Street Revival was the first in which tongues were manifest since Apostolic times. That was just poor historical knowledge, as other Spirit-filled and tongues manifesting revivals have broken out throughout Church history. The early 1900s saw several outbreaks, including in India and Texas, although certainly the Azusa Street Revival became the most famous and influential of all.

In any case, the YWAM PPS is more elaborate, and better thought out than our original Little Five Points one. The standard kit includes a folding table to keep hand-outs, tracts and other materials, a large attractive sign stretched out along a triangular PCV frame with "prayer station" in bold letters. It also inclued ministry vests with the slogan, "prayer changes things" printed on them, plus a training manual. The manual suggests that besides the prayer intercessors, each station have designated persons who hand out flyers to passersby inviting them to prayer. It is all quite attractive and effective.[2] Most importantly, there is provision for follow up, so that the person prayed over can be guided to a church and discipled. Several YWAM PPSs did especially good service in the immediate aftermath of the 9/11 terrorist attack in comforting and praying for New Yorkers.

Mr. Sovaca began marketing this kit all over the world and has sold and shipped over a thousand of them to many different countries. The YWAM kits have made a strong impact "Down Under" in Australia and New Zealand. Their various Prayer Station websites are full of great testimonials. Here is one particularly charming testimony addressed to an PPS intercessor from New Zealand.

Dear David,

I would like to give thanks to God for using you to answer our prayers. Who would imagine that God would bring us to Auckland, New Zealand (on a short holiday) to answer our prayers through you?

---

[1] See brief description in YWAM site under "History." At http://www.ywamny.org/prayerstations/

[2] Note the YWAM PPS pictures at their wesite: http://prayerstations.org/

Vivian and I have been married for 5 years and we were trying to start our family for the past one and the half year. We knew in our hearts that He would provide a child in his time. We prayed between ourselves, and close family members did too. After a while, we became slightly anxious. Then, when Vivian was diagnosed to have a polycystic ovarian condition which makes it harder to conceive, she started taking some hormone replacement therapy. After half a year on that medication, we stopped because there were no positive results.

We decided to wait for His promises. There were many occasions when we lost confidence, thinking that it was His plan for us NOT to have a family.

David, when you prayed for us that day in Nov. '04 - at the Prayer Station on Queen Street, Auckland—Vivian felt God's peace once again. She had always wanted someone like you to pray for us.

Two months later we discovered God had answered your prayers that night - and she was two months pregnant. Now she is into the 7 month of pregnancy. Everything has been good. Mother and child are doing well. In the earlier days, there were so many things that we did or ate that may threaten the pregnancy (as we did not know that she was pregnant). God has been so good. He blessed us with this child despite all circumstances medically or otherwise.

Thank you for your prayer. You have helped to move God's hand in providing this baby for us. Praise God for your prayers. Thank you once again.

Bernard and Vivian Lee Singapore[3]

The "Prayer Station" manual that comes with the kit includes several CDs about the ministry and is long on instructions about assembling the table and banner and its positioning. "Be careful not to locate it in a windy area, as it may sail away." But it is short on instructions on healing or intercessory prayer. Although Mr. Sovaca was raised in a Pentecostal household, and in his testimony openly values his Pentecostal heritage, he mentions nothing about using the gifts of the Spirit or their usefulness in praying for others. That avoids controversy with Evangelical brethren who do not believe in the gifts of the Spirit, but it also weakens the value of the training by not encouraging praying in the power of the Spirit.

In 2016 Mr. Sovaca separated from YWAM, as Mercy Ships had earlier done. Mr. Sovaca relocated to Jupiter, Florida, and formed a corporation

---

[3]From the New Zealand Prayer Station webpage. Accessed April 14, 2017. http://across.co.nz/PSNewLifeSpore.html

to concentrate on selling and shipping the Prayer Station kits. But truthfully, it is puzzling as to why he moved his group to Florida. New York is perhaps the capital of American Nones, and a terrific place for multiple ongoing PPSs.

Mr. Sovaca filed for and received a trademark registration for the phrase "prayer station." He wants no other group to use that phrase without his permission. His rational is that he must monitor and ensure the quality of such PPSs that use that phrase. My lawyer assured me that his trademark would not stand up in court if challenged in view of the St. Patrick's OSL group earlier use. Further, many church groups had been using the prayer station phrase even before our St. Patrick's group to indicate prayer spaces within churches for prayer (see introduction). One only needs to google "prayer station" in the image mode to be led to countless church sites that use the phrase.

I believe Mr. Sovaca's use of the trademark is a disservice to the Church as a whole, as the phrase is the most natural for this type of ministry. I also believe Christians should stay out of secular courts (1 Cor 6:5-7) and I have no taste or plans of litigation on this issue. In this work I have been careful to use the acronym PPS as an accommodation to Mr. Sovaca, and would suggest that new PPSs perhaps chose a different phrase, such as "prayer place" or "prayer kiosk," etc.

I don't want to finish on this negative note, so I must repeat that overall the "Prayer Station" kits are of high quality and very attractive, and in many places are doing yeoman work in effective evangelization and healing prayer.

Before we describe the HOTS ministry, perhaps the boldest and most effective PPS ministry of all, let me mention a relatively new manifestation of the PPS, called "Prayer Stop." It is focused on "presenting the Gospel" in an Evangelical understanding, and unfortunately mostly ignores healing prayer.[4]

The founder, Darrel Rundus, was a businessman who built a large and successful newspaper marketing company. In the course of his career, he became expert at communication and persuasion. In 2002, at the height of his business success, he received Jesus and became passionately Evangelical.[5] He sold his business and then dedicated all the skills and lessons

---

[4]Web page with a sketch of its founding and goals is at: https://www.prayerstop.org/pages/home

[5]His witness at: Frontline Apologetics "Darrel Rundus(the multimillionaire from Dallas) Witness." Posted Aug. 29, 2005. http://frontlineapologetics.blogspot.com/-2005/08/darrel-rundus-multimillionaire-from.html

he learned about communication, for the sake of the Gospel. He helped organize a large Gospel Boot Camp for a major Texas mega-church, and then went on to found the Prayer Stop ministry.

Mr. Rundus has, just like Sovaca's group, packaged a kiosk type setup with an attractive sign and small table. Some of the Prayer Stop kits are "premium" and more elaborate than the kits from Sovaca's company. The premium Prayer Stop kit includes ten each of t-shirts, hats, ministry vests, note pads, plus two chairs, and even bibles to give away. There is a smaller and less expensive kit, and the attractive kiosk can be bought by itself.[6]

Mr. Rundus provides a training CD with every kit, "Empowered." It is all about presenting the Gospel of salvation clearly and soul winning. Actually, most of the teachings can be accessed on YouTube.[7] The intercessors are trained to use various "ice breakers," questions to begin conversations with passersby and then present the Gospel to them with further questions. The Prayer Stop intercessor then offers to pray for their intention. The intercessors carry notepads and are trained to list the supplicant's requests so that they do not forget any of the petitions.

Naturally many of the requests are for healing for themselves or others. The technique used for healing prayer is Fundamentalist-Evangelical. The supplicant and intercessors hold hands, and lift up prayers to the Lord for the intentions one by one. No command healing is used, nor is the laying on of hands on an afflicted area encouraged.

From my charismatic perspective, I find Mr. Rundus' teaching on soul winning very good, and will incorporate some of his tips into my next PPS outings. His Prayer Stop is the first PPS ministry to my knowledge to have gained access to the interior of a shopping mall, an ideal place for the PPS. His good business relations are probably why he was able to gain such access.

---

[6]https://www.prayerstop.org/collections/kiosks-kits
[7]https://www.youtube.com/watch?v=npTd6E656Ek&t=23s

# 7

# Chairs as the public prayer station

Unlike Sovaca's PPS, or the Prayer Stop, the HOTS (Healing On The Streets) ministry is openly Pentecostal and unrestrained about the public use of the gifts of the Spirit, or the laying on of hands. Its founder and director, Mark Marx, was discipled at an Elim (Pentecostal) church and later associated as evangelist with several Vineyard churches in the UK. HOTS assertiveness in proclaiming the healing Gospel and bringing salvation to many is proving effective, even in the cold spiritual atmosphere of the UK and Scandinavia where church attendance is low.

Mark was born in Capetown, South Africa, in 1957, from a Chinese mother and Jewish father.[1] By age four, Marx's father fell into alcoholism, but remained sober enough to run a small grocery business. He decided he would do better in the UK, and emigrated to England and brought Mark with him, Mark's mother stayed in South Africa. Mark never saw her again.

Unusually, Mark was enrolled in a Catholic primary school, and attended school chapel where he felt an awe and peace about the place. He was not allowed to receive Holy Communion since he was not baptized, and he felt that lack. Mark was then sent to an Anglican boarding school. There he was offered confirmation into Anglicanism but declined because he was not yet absolutely sure of the truth of the Gospel.

Mark became a successful interior decorator. But like his father, fell into depression and alcoholism. Providentially, Marx had a friend who

---

[1] The biographical information on the Rev. Marx is taken from his fine autobiography, and description of the HOTS ministry, Mark Marx, *Stepping into the Impossible*, (Maidstone, UK: River, 2015).

pestered him to come to church. He finally did so, to an Elim church. As he stepped into the building he again felt the presence of God and was awed by the spirit of worship he found there.

Mark returned to that church and on the third time the Anglican minister, Trevor Dearing and his wife, were guest ministers.[2] Mark responded to their invitation to come forward for salvation. When Mrs. Dearing laid hands on him, he was slain in the spirit and fell to the floor.[3] During "carpet time" the Lord spoke to him and told him that his long-time grieving over his father's alcoholism was healed. When he arose he discovered that indeed it was.

Mark became a "charismaniac," reading the Bible until the wee hours, attending church as often as he could, and devouring books about the Spirit-filled life. He also began to pray for the healing of others, especially elderly persons for whom he felt a special compassion. That produced meager results, but he persisted in it. In this Mark repeated the pattern that John Wimber experienced early in his ministry. Wimber prayed for months for various healings, believing God's word, but having no positive results, but then experienced a major breakthrough.[4]

At the Elim church, and later at a Vineyard fellowship, Mark sought to learn everything he could about evangelization. His enthusiasm and dedication were noted and he became part of a Vineyard staff as an evangelist. Mark learned that some of the Pentecostal evangelists used leg and arm extensions for the healing of back problems, and he began using those procedures. (There is no indication that he learned this from the Hunter Ministry materials.)

At the Vineyard church he attended, there was a street drama team that did skits to present the Gospel. Mark joined them for a try. One skit, which Mark took part in, presented an "unsaved" person as a chicken without his head. It was a total flop, and Mark felt embarrassed for the well-intentioned evangelist team.

The evangelistic team turned to "sketch board evangelism." In this technique an evangelist uses an easel with a large sketch board and writes out sentences that explain the Gospel.[5] Mark tried this for himself with much frustration and no salvations. He prayed, "God, there must be a bet-

---

[2] The Rev. Dearing was a major figure in the Anglican charismatic revival, and known especially for his exorcism ministry. See, Trevor Dearing, *Supernatural Superpowers* (Plainfield: Logos International, 1977).

[3] Marx, *Stepping*. 25.

[4] John Wimber *Power Healing*. (San Francesco: Harper Collins, 1987).

[5] See this form of evangelization done in a Youtube video: https://www.youtube.com/watch?v=hyuuh6bpnjA

ter way than this."⁶ Immediately, he tore away the sheet of Gospel passages and wrote in bold letters, "HEALINGS AND MIRACLES HERE." With a megaphone he called out to the passersby, "Anyone needs healing?"

A man came up and requested to be free of his cigarette addiction. He had tried everything medical and nothing worked. Mark prayed for him and instantly his desire for a cigarette left. He crumped up his box of cigarettes and threw them down. Mark took up his megaphone again and offered to pray for freedom from the cigarette addiction. A line formed of those wanting such prayer, and not too long after, a pile of crumpled cigarette boxes had formed.

But one who came up asked "Well, I suffer from arthritis. Can God heal me of arthritis?" That man was healed.⁷ Mark understood that praying for healing was the way to do effective street evangelization. Mark had re-invented the PPS without using the word "prayer station" or anything like it. But it had the essential elements. A spot on a public thoroughfare, a sign (on an easel), and an invitation to prayer.

As Mark regularly led his prayer team to the streets this combination of megaphone, easel and sketch board, "signs and wonders" followed. People were often slain in the spirit and healed of emotional and physical maladies. Of course the effectiveness of Mark's team was enhanced by the fact the volunteers were from a Spirit-filled Vineyard church and understood the workings of the gifts of the Sprit. They knew for instance, to stand behind a person who was being prayed for in case they "fell under the power."⁸

In one town where his team went to model the PPS for a local Vineyard, it had been raining heavily, and there were pools of water on the streets and sidewalks. An elderly lady came up and asked healing for arthritis of the neck. Mark prayed a quick mental prayer, "Lord don't let her fall and get wet." He then laid hands on her neck. She was "half" slain in the Spirit. That is, her upper body went limp and she bent over and her hands touched her toes, but her legs stood firm, like the legs of a sleeping horse. This kept her from falling and getting soaked. Mark preached the Gospel to the curious crowd as they watched. When she came to, she was completely healed.⁹

---

⁶Marx, *Stepping*, 40.
⁷Ibid. 42.
⁸On why some persons are injured when they fall under the power of God see, William De Arteaga, *Anglican Pentecostal*, "Energies of God," Posted: Nov. 8, 2013. http://anglicalpentecostal.blogspot.com/2013/11/energies-of-god-from-fallings-to.html
⁹Marx, *Stepping*, 40-41.

Mark's success as evangelist led him to different towns and cities in the UK, and even some overseas invitations. But a hiatus. In 1998 Mark felt a call from the Lord to live in Northern Ireland. This was verified by a personal prophecy from Cindy Jacobs, the famous American charismatic evangelist and prophet who was visiting the UK at the time.

Mark and his family moved to Coleraine, a town just inland from the north coast. This was when Northern Ireland was undergoing the "troubles," i.e., civil war between Catholics and Protestants. Mark got a job as window salesman and traveled without incident in the most contentious and bombed out parts of the Northern Ireland, a miracle in itself. In Coleraine he and his family joined a Vineyard church, but without ministry responsibilities.

After several years, the pastor there asked Mark to lead a team in street evangelism. This time, when Mark went out with his team, he took several chairs for persons waiting in line to be healed. The ministry's very first supplicant was an Indian woman with one leg noticeably shorter than the other. That was dispatched quickly to the amazement of various witnesses. The Coleraine, Vineyard street ministry developed a strong anointing and was very successful. Mark was asked to lead and teach at other UK Vineyard churches about this ministry.

In 2005 Mark was invited to do healing a conference for UK Vineyard leaders. At the end of the conference, attendees went out to do ministry. One participant had a small banner with the single word "healing" printed on it. It worked surprisingly well to attract passersby.

Back in Coleraine, Mark was asked to field a "healing on the streets" event, as it was now called, once a week. The church bought six sturdy folding chairs, a large banner with the word "Healing," a collapsible pole and stand, and a portable PA system. Members who wanted to be on the team were trained on two consecutive Sunday evenings.

At first launch, the team kneeled in a circle to pray. Everyone felt a special anointing fall. (It has become part of the HOTS playbook to kneel and pray at the beginning of their PPS events.) Unlike most other PPS prayer intercessors, HOTS prayer intercessors most often kneel next to the seated supplicants.

*Chairs as the public prayer station 61*

Note the banner, folding wooden chairs and aqua kneelers. The building in the back is the Coleraine City Hall, rebuilt after being demolished by an IRA bomb in 1995. Picture used by permission

The Coleraine Vineyard HOTS team went out every Saturday, to the same place, in front of the town hall. This was consciously done to build up a healing atmosphere in the area. Miracles after another piled up and ever more people came. After the fourth week the HOTS ministry made the local paper, *The Chronicle*, as a very positive lead story, "Miracles on our Street."[10] The pattern was set. The team would assemble and kneel together for prayer. They would bring folding chairs, a large banner, leaflets to hand out and a portable PA system to play soothing Christian music. Some team members would pass out leaflets inviting the public to prayer, as in the Sovaca's teams. Ministry was carried out rain or shine.

As supplicants sat, a team gathered and knelt around the seated supplicant to pray. They first call on the Holy Spirit to reveal himself to the supplicant. When they sense the supplicant has made a connection with God, they ask permission to lay hands on the person for prayer. They always affirm that God loves them. The teams often minister in the gifts of the Spirit, words of wisdom, knowledge, etc. John Wimber, the founder of the Vineyard churches, urged prayer intercessors to keep their eyes open during prayer and note the bodily manifestations of the Holy Spirit's work, such as fluttering eyelids.[11] The HOTS teams are trained to follow this pattern.

---

[10]Ibid., See chapter 10 "Healing on the Streets model," for details.
[11]Ibid. 105. See Wimber *Power Healing*.

The ministry teams are also trained to use the command mode of healing, a form not stressed by Wimber, but central to the Hunter's mode of ministry. But by the 1990s command healing had spread among many charismatic Believers. The HOTS teams consciously operate in the full "authority of the Believer," which again was stressed by the Hunters. Another commonality with the Hunter method is that the HOTS teams ask the supplicant to gently test for healing after the prayers are finished. This would indicate either that the healing is complete or the need for further prayer. There is no indication that these prayer forms and procedures were learned *directly* from the Hunter's ministry materials, although some of it may have been.[12] Finally, the supplicant is given an envelope which includes an invitation to their church, and the booklet "Why Jesus?" which explains the Gospel of salvation. As is common to the PPS, there is a constant evangelical byproduct of their healing prayers. Mark wrote:

> "When we go out onto the streets, God's presence goes with us. We become a church without walls, where people who wouldn't normally walk into a church building can experience God. They don't have to come and sit on a chair for prayers to encounter him. Just walking past, they can experience God's presence and power."[13]

In one case a paralyzed woman was brought in a wheel chair by her family. Nearby a skeptical crowd watched. Mark laid hands on her and felt the power of God go through her – even the wheel chair was vibrating. The lady said "I want to walk.' She did. One of the skeptics watching came over and said "I've seen that woman healed, I want to become a Christian now!"[14]

To summarize: HOTS is a superb manifestation of the PPS ministry. Perhaps the boldest and most effective of all we have seen. Unfortunately HOTS is not as widespread as the YWAM variety, and mostly limited to the UK and to several countries in Europe and Scandinavia. It has some American stations, but the HOTS model has not become widespread in the "colonies." It is not clear why not. It seems a perfect ministry for Americans, who are too often overweight, and sitting for prayer rather than standing would be a great idea. However, one HOTS station in San Diego seems to be doing fine. Here is a wonderful account of how an atheist recently came to Christ there.

> "An Atheist walked past avoiding us (twice!) Just all twisted over, really hunched, his knee was almost pointing inwards and his back was curving

---

[12][Marx] *Healing*, 6.
[13]Marx, *Stepping,* 138.
[14]Ibid. 127.

in. He had two accidents five years ago that put him out of work. When I meet him he says 'I'm an atheist, I don't believe in God.'... I tell him what has he got to lose, and he shrugs and sits down saying 'Well, if you can get me back into work tomorrow!'

First thing, his knee (the most painful part) gets healed and then down further his foot. He stands up and nearly cries. He sits down and says 'Either you're hypnotizing me or brainwashing me or you're converting me. My knee is better.' So he asks for prayer for his back. Then he stands up straight and chokes back tears. He says 'I haven't been able to do that for two years. You guys are converting me.'

He sits down, we pray again, and then he stands up and says loud to everyone around (including our German friend) 'I haven't stood up straight for two years. I don't believe in this stuff! These guys are turning me around.'

I talk to him about Jesus and he says, 'I never talk to anyone about God because I don't believe in him. But he healed me. I'm going to look into this.' So we arranged to get a coffee this week."[15]

---

[15] From Mark Marx's timeline on Facebook. Posted 4/7/2018

# Part III

# Starting a Public Prayer Station

# 8

# Ready, shoot, aim!

Some people might think that starting a PPS involves much planning. Really, some planning, but not much. More important is to pray for the Lord's direction on this as in any other ministry, but the PPS is not rocket science. In this ministry it is best to use the management strategy known as, "ready, shoot, aim." That is, do some planning, go and do it, and then adjust, correct any mistakes, and make it better.

The fundamentals are having a church or bible study prayer team that includes some persons with experience in praying for others, and some sort of sign or symbol indicating this is the place you pray for them. You can make up some sign like we did, buy a kit, or you can go to one of the many sign printing stores that now are in every community. You may wish to add a few chairs for the supplicants, the way the HOTS people do. I believe it is also important to have a prayerful send-off and commissioning by your pastor and congregation as we did at St. Patrick's. That gives you spiritual prayer cover and authority. None of that is difficult nor does it demand extensive planning.

Recently, a Facebook buddy drew my attention to a PPS tent ministry that was birthed several years ago in Erie, Pennsylvania. Michael and Kara De John led a home group there as part of a charismatic church. They wanted to impact and bless the people who came to Erie's "Ribfest and Music Festival" that takes place yearly at the end of May. They set up a tent, called it "There's Love in Erie" and handed out balloons and other giveaways for children. As the people came by they offered prayers. It was very successful, with several persons giving their lives to the Lord and many healings. This year (2018) will be third outing at the Ribfest, and the group plans other local outings. The lesson is that a successful PPS is as easy as that, a small group of persons who want to share the love of Jesus and pray for others.[1]

Intercessors ready to pounce with prayer (Mrs. Kara De John is at the far right). Picture used by permission of the DeJohn's.

Specific training is also good, but as I have indicated, we started at St. Patrick's with persons who knew how to prayer for others in church, but had no specific instructions on how to do it on the streets. It was not a difficult transition. The "Prayer Stop" ministry has, as mentioned, some excellent training on leading a person to Christ, as do many other ministries. On reflection, I wish I had done that sort of training with the St. Patrick's team.

Other things are secondary, but good too. It is a great idea to have a table for free literature and Bibles, but some city jurisdictions may not allow it, or you may need a permit. If you have a large team of volunteers, more than six, you might add designated flyer distributors, as the Sovaca and HOTS folks do. Also good is some sort of follow up literature, as the letter and booklet handed out by the HOTS ministry. I would suggest that in that letter you list local churches, including your own, that you can recommend for the person to continue in his or her Christian walk.

Now of course, I suggest learning command prayer and the Hunter package of arm and leg extensions, as so many people have one sort of back problem or another. But some Christians are still wary of the com-

---

[1] The group's Facebook page at: http://www.facebook.com/groups/1578653709050683

mand mode of healing prayer and want to use the petition mode. That is OK – less effective, and more time consuming, but OK. Other Christians think the whole Hunter method is "cultic" because it is not in the Bible. That is an unfortunate attitude, as a whole lot of stuff is not specifically in the Bible, as for instance the institution of Sunday School.

All of which is to say one can start a PPS with a quite traditional attitude towards prayer and still be a great success. However, I have some trouble believing that a convinced fundamentalist/cessationist, who believes that the age of miraculous healing is gone, would have much success. Can you imagine their prayers? "Oh Lord help this person endure this suffering patiently… and grant him peace of mind." No kidding, that sort of stuff is in older ministry manuals modeling various prayers for the sick and hospital visitations. The Prayer Stop ministry fudges on this issue and recommends offering only hand-holding petition prayers for healing. But I noticed in one of their Youtube videos a young man bending over and laying hands on a person's ankles – good for him.

Don't let Satan con you in not starting a PPS or indefinitely delaying it for further training. Remember "ready, shoot, aim." If you have an experienced intercessor prayer team, GO. Clobber together a PPS sign, or buy one, ask your church to bless the group and GO! Ask the Lord to show you a spot, or a coming public event, such as a craft fair, and GO! Suggest to your team they read the Hunter book, *How to Heal the Sick*, or look at the Hunter YouTube videos, to get additional training on healing. But GO even if they have not had the chance. I do a one-day training workshop on all of this, and would love to come to your church, but the workshop is not necessary, just GO!

If your church can buy the PPS kit from the former YWAM folks, or Prayer Stop, do that. Both are really nice, and GO as soon as you get the kit. I learned to be thrifty (some would say cheap) in my years as the minister to a mostly poor Hispanic congregation, and prefer to do things inexpensively. One can make an effective PPS for practically nothing – there are plenty of unused real estate signs lying around. The ministry vests can be bought at Walmart or Amazon for about than $6 apiece. One can customize them to your church with "iron on" decals sold at Office Depot that you design on your computer. In fact, inexpensive name tags will do as well. Your church probably has a stack of them lying around unused. A small table for tracts and other materials can be had at practically any yard sale or flea market for a few dollars. Most computer sign shops will do a nice banner for you inexpensively. In any case, just GO!

If you belong to a mega church, why not try the "mother of all PPS." Start with the Sovaca kit, add six chairs and a large banner like HOTS, bullhorns, have plenty of volunteers for flyers, add music - perhaps a live band, and as the Christmas carol goes, "twelve maids a dancing and a partridge in a pear tree." Hey, that would be fun and bring in local TV coverage.

Seriously, go consistently at the same spot so that a spiritual atmosphere builds up in the area and people in distress know where to go for prayer. Some will pass by snickering the first time, but come when their troubles mount.

In any case, GO!

# Resources

## Books on the healing ministry and PPS

Hunter, Charles, and Frances Hunter. *How to Heal the Sick.* Kingwood: Hunter Books, 1981.

———. *Handbook for Healing.* Kingwood: Hunter Books, 1987. These books are a wonderful resource for the PPS ministry. It would be good for every prayer team should read at least the first one, and have the other as a resource.

———. "How to Heal the Sick." Youtube: https://www.youtube.com/watch?v=GdJwTqGkf38

Laubach, Frank. *The Game With Minutes.* Westwood: Fleming H Revel, 1956. Modern editions in print. This work is a classic of prayer, and especially pertinent to the PPS intercessor. It models, among other things, how to "bombard" passersby with prayers and blessings.

MacNutt, Frances. *Healing.* Notre Dame: Ave Maria 1974. A wonderful general introduction to healing prayer.

[Marx, Mark], *Healing on the Streets: Training Manual.* Coleraine, UK: Causeway Coast, 2015. Available only through HOTS ministry in the UK. Pricy but excellent.

Marx, Mark. *Stepping into the Impossible: The Story of Healing on the Streets* Maidstone, UK: River Publishing, 2015. Available on Amazon as print or Kindle. Terrific resource for the PPS.

Sanford, Agnes. *The Healing Light.* Plainsfield: Logos International, 1967. 1st edition in 1947. A classic on healing prayer.

Wimber, John, and Kevin Springer. *Power Healing.* San Francisco: Harper Collins, 1987.

———. *Power Evangelism.* San Francisco: Harper Collins, 1986.

## Books and articles on the exorcism/deliverance ministry

Randy Clark. *The Biblical Guidebook to Deliverance.* Lake Mary: Charisma House, 2015.

De Arteaga, William. "The Rev. John L. Nevius: The Holy Spirit Gives a Lesson in Chinese." *Pneuma Review.* Posted May 10, 2014.

http://pneumareview.com/the-rev-john-l-nevius-the-holy-spirit-gives-a-lesson-in-chinese/

———. "If it Quacks Like a Duck: The Discovery of the Demonic by Secular Psychiatrists," *Anglican Pentecostal*. Posted, June 6, 2017. http://anglicalpentecostal.blogspot,com/2017/06/if-it-quacks-like-duck-discovery-of-html.

Frank and Ida Mae Hammond. *Pigs in the Parlor.* Kirkwood: Impact Books, 1973. A Pentecostal view. Very useful.

Frances MacNutt. *Deliverance from Evil Spirits.* Grand Rapids: Chosen, 1995. Marvelously balanced and intelligent view of the demonic and the Christian's responsibility to do deliverance ministry as part of the healing ministry.

## Made to order banners

These can be gotten inexpensively in many print and banner shops that dot the country. In my home town of Canton, GA, there were several shops less than 15 minutes' drive that could supply nicely done all-weather banners

Here is an excellent national site:
https://www.churchbanners.com/

Official "Prayer Station" signs and kits
https://prayerstations.org/

"Prayer Stop" ministry resources:
https://www.prayerstop.org/pages/home

You Tube training video for "Prayer Stop":
https://www.youtube.com/watch?v=S0dcdByMkrM

"Soul winning" scripts:
Very effective and useful laminated card for intercessors who are shy or inexperienced in leading others to the Lord. From the ministry of Rodney Howard-Brown at:
http://store.revival.com/gospel-soulwinning-scripts-100-english/

## Bibles

At Christianbook.com there are new NIV Bibles available for as little as $2.00. The same site sells a packet of 10 Gospels of John for $6.00. If you can find a lower price, go for it.

## Suggested follow up letter

Dear Friend:

You have just been touched by God's healing and miracle power thru one of our intercessors. We want you to know that God loves you, and wants His touch and love to be a constant factor in your life.

If you felt a healing take place, please do not discontinue taking medication until you get an OK from your doctor.

We will be here on a regular basis and you are more than welcome to return for more prayer, and to bring along someone who also needs prayer. We suggest that if you do not now go to church regularly, you begin to do so, and that you make daily Bible reading a part of your life. Biblegateway.com has several Bible reading plans for you on their website. You are most welcome to come to our church, xxxxxxxxx, at number, street, town, where effective healing prayer is offered at every service. But there are also many good churches close by.

(A more detailed letter is found in *Healing on the Streets: Training Manual* cited above.)

# Appendix

# ACTS 29

**NEWSLETTER OF THE EPISCOPAL RENEWAL MINISTRIES**

DEDICATED TO THE RENEWAL OF PEOPLE AND PARISHES THROUGH:
APOSTOLIC TEACHING • BIBLICAL PREACHING
HISTORIC WORSHIP • CHARISMATIC EXPERIENCE

MAY 1988

## Ministry at Little Five Points

by William L. de Arteaga

Visitors last summer to Atlanta's Little Five Points district may have seen a most unusual scene. Amidst the counter-culture youths and street people of the area was a group of ordinary-looking persons praying and laying hands on passers-by. Each prayer intercessor wore a name badge upon which was written his or her first name and the words "OSL Prayer Intercessor." Nearby was a real estate sign that had been painted over and lettered in bright red with the words "prayer station." An observer could not help noticing a chubby middle-aged man with a graying mustache near the sign, asking those who caught his eye: "Would you like some prayer today?" Most people simply smiled and politely declined, and a few would impolitely decline. Some found the request humorous and walked away giggling.

But a steady stream of passers-by did accept the invitation to receive prayer. When they did, several members of the ministry team would assist in praying.

This strange scene, of Christians willing to make fools of themselves for the Lord, was the fruit of one of the newest ministries of the Episcopal Church in the Atlanta area. It is a street ministry of prayer evangelism, based on the concept of "power evangelism" popularized by John Wimber (of Vineyard Fellowships in California) and David Pytches (a Church of England bishop with an Anglicanized version of Wimber's technique).

The Little Five Points area of Atlanta is the center of counter-culture in the Southeast. Within a few blocks of this famous crossroads there congregates a mix of unusual groups. Older persons from the "hippie" era of the 1960's mingle with the current generation of rebellious adolescents, youngsters of the "punk rock" culture. Political radicals can be heard selling their ideological wares and there is a high proportion of "out-of-the-closet" homosexuals who feel free to express their tendencies in this community. One can spot among the residents a sprinkling of witches, Satan-worshipers and adherents of oriental cults. Many of Atlanta's street people come to this area because of the large soup kitchens and shelters found close by. The offbeat residents of this area, together with the craft shops, restaurants and specialty book stores, make Little Five Points one of the most popular tourist spots in Atlanta.

This ministry had its origins as an outreach activity of the Order of St. Luke's chapter at St. Patrick's Episcopal Church in Dunnwoody, one of Atlanta's most affluent suburbs. St. Patrick's is noted as a beacon to charismatic Episcopalians

(continued on page 2)

Page 1 of the May, 1988 issue of *Acts 29*

www.ingramcontent.com/pod-product-compliance
Lightning Source LLC
Chambersburg PA
CBHW071239090426
42736CB00014B/3138